GOING
RED

GOING RED

THE TWO MILLION VOTERS WHO WILL ELECT THE NEXT PRESIDENT—AND HOW CONSERVATIVES CAN WIN THEM

ED MORRISSEY

CROWN
FORUM
NEW YORK

Copyright © 2016 by Ed Morrissey

All rights reserved.
Published in the United States by Crown Forum,
an imprint of the Crown Publishing Group,
a division of Penguin Random House LLC, New York.
www.crownpublishing.com

CROWN FORUM with colophon is a registered
trademark of Penguin Random House LLC.

Library of Congress Cataloging-in-Publication Data
is available upon request.

ISBN 978-1-101-90566-1
eBook ISBN 978-1-101-90567-8

PRINTED IN THE UNITED STATES OF AMERICA

Jacket design by Tal Goretsky

10   9   8   7   6   5   4   3   2   1

First Edition

To Marcia

For Kayla, Elizabeth, David, and Missy

CONTENTS

GOING
RED

INTRODUCTION
THE ILLUSION SHATTERS

M ore than three years ago, the hopes and delusions of the Republican Party collapsed in a shocking defeat that few on the Right saw coming. And I had a ringside seat at the disaster.

It was election day 2012 at the Southern California studios of Hugh Hewitt's conservative talk radio show, and a palpable sense of optimism was buzzing in the air. At the desks outside the main studio, bloggers and analysts were hunched over their laptops, looking for the latest hint of the outcome and occasionally slipping in and out of the studio to share data. Inside the studio, I was with five on-air commentators, crowded around Hugh's desk, narrating the election and preparing to celebrate victory. Early in the evening, we jostled elbows for time on the microphones, giving breathless updates and sunny predictions based on the reports of GOP sources who had told us to expect victory.

But when the polls began to close, the smiles on our faces disappeared. Early losses in states such as Michigan (where Mitt Romney's father once served as governor), New Hampshire, and Pennsylvania in the first fifty minutes of national returns soured the mood in the studio. The news that Romney won back North Carolina lifted our spirits, but within moments, it was reported that Iowa had pulled for Obama. And, at 8:17 p.m. Pacific time, we stared at one another across the desk as all of the major networks called Ohio for Obama.* This was the surest sign of disaster; no Republican had ever won the presidency without Ohio.

With Ohio in Obama's column, CBS News[1] felt confident enough to call the election: incumbent president Barack Obama would cruise to victory, they reported. And the news got worse from there. Despite believing that they had leads in swing states such as Florida and Virginia, the Romney campaign lost those and others as well. Not only had Obama won reelection, he had won all but two of the states he had pulled away from the GOP in 2008.

We sat in the studio for hours, dazed, trying to comprehend how everything had gone so wrong. None of us had seen this coming. How did Republicans miss what looked like a golden opportunity to prevail?

In the twelve months leading up to that moment, the election had looked to be anyone's game. Romney limped out of a brutal primary season that saw more debates and less clarity of message than any previous cycle. GOP voters had expressed a desire for something other than the usual next-in-line progression of presidential nominees, but Romney had burned through his campaign's supply of cash to prevail over challenger Rick Santorum, who by that time hadn't held office in five years.

---

* Fox News would debate that call for another twenty minutes.

On the Democrats' side of the aisle, the picture wasn't much rosier, thanks to a sluggish economy and a sense that trouble was brewing on the foreign policy front, with the collapse of Libya and the sacking of the American consulate in Benghazi. Dogged by low approval ratings, the president began avoiding the beat reporters at the White House, opting instead to focus attention on friendlier interviews* with local news stations and entertainment outlets like *People* magazine and *Entertainment Tonight*.[2]

Republicans smelled blood in the water, believing that 2012 would give them an opportunity to unseat Obama. After losing in 2008, the Republican Party had picked up momentum in their 2010 midterm sweep, which seemed ready to carry over into an election-night victory. Their hopes surged even higher after the first presidential debate, in which Romney outclassed the incumbent, who seemed distracted and peevish.

National polling had supported this optimism, too. Two weeks ahead of the election, pollsters from CNN, Fox News, and *Politico* put the election at a tie—but outlets like the Associated Press, NPR, and Gallup were starting to give Romney the edge. Romney himself was so confident, in fact, that he bragged on Election Day that he'd only written one speech to use later that night.[3]

One wonders, then, how long it took for the Republican contender to start writing a different speech once the results

---

* "It's a curious election," said MSNBC's Joe Scarborough, sighing derisively, on *Morning Joe* on August 16, 2012: "Where do I go to get my weighty interview? I go to [*Entertainment Tonight* host] Nancy O'Dell."

started coming in. Team Romney's plan had relied on the belief that he could take back swing states like Virginia, Ohio, New Hampshire, Florida, Colorado, Wisconsin, and North Carolina from Obama. But with the exception of a narrow win for Romney in North Carolina, each of these states lined up in the Democrats' column. In Ohio, the state that effectively decided the race, exit polls showed a turnout model that closely mirrored Obama's eight-point advantage from four years earlier.[4]

Republicans had assumed that their surge in the 2010 midterms meant voters had rejected the Obama agenda, and Obama himself. They assumed that the turnout model of 2008, which favored Democrats by seven points, had been neutralized. And, most critical, they assumed that the conversation in national media directly reflected the concerns of voters on the ground, thanks to the proliferation of communications and news access in the Internet age.

Those assumptions turned out to be the key factor in Mitt Romney's loss. As the Republican National Committee (RNC) itself concluded, Obama ran "a national campaign like a local election."[5] Much of the analysis focused on how the president used social media and advanced technology to push his message—an effort Republicans tried to emulate in 2012—but they missed how the Obama campaign used social media not just to message, but also to get to know voters in critical battlegrounds. Republicans ran a thirty-thousand-foot messaging campaign on national talking points, while the Obama campaign had ambassadors on the ground discussing how Obama would address their specific concerns.

Practically everyone has heard the old axiom "All politics

is local." Republicans forgot that key point in 2008 and 2012 and paid a steep price.

THE AUTOPSY

What went wrong? In December 2012, Republican Party chair Reince Priebus launched what the media termed an "autopsy" of the failed presidential campaign, from the perspective of the GOP's involvement. The official name for the report sounded somewhat more optimistic: the "Growth and Opportunity Project." The one-hundred-page treatise on the failings of the GOP included this telling conclusion about the last several election cycles:[6]

> The GOP today is a tale of two parties. One of them, the gubernatorial wing, is growing and successful. The other, the federal wing, is increasingly marginalizing itself, and unless changes are made, it will be increasingly difficult for Republicans to win another presidential election in the near future.[7]

Lost in the hand-wringing about the 2012 result is the reality of Republican dominance at the state level. In 2015, the party had total control of thirty state legislatures, compared with only eleven for Democrats.[8] On top of that, thirty-one states had GOP governors during the same time.[9] The number of Electoral College votes from states with Republican governors comes to 315—more than enough for a comfortable win in a presidential election.

The report found that Republicans have some skill in reaching voters in state and local elections, yet they seem unable to marshal their power in presidential contests. The issue becomes even more acute when one considers four states that in 2012 had Republican governors and GOP-controlled state legislatures but still voted for Obama:

- Florida—29 electoral votes
- Ohio—18 electoral votes
- Virginia—13 electoral votes
- Wisconsin—10 electoral votes

Flipping just these four states in 2012 would have swung seventy Electoral College votes to the Republicans, giving Romney the victory, 276 to 262.*

Hugh Hewitt argues that Obama's near-sweep of the 2012 swing states distorts what actually was a close, and winnable, election. "It was a narrow loss, but one that became obvious early" in the night, he recalls. "One hundred thousand votes in Florida, 100,000 votes in Virginia, 100,000 in Ohio, 120,000 in Colorado, and it goes the other way," Hewitt notes. "But as soon as we lost Florida or Ohio or Virginia, we knew we were doomed."

Wisconsin governor Scott Walker puts his finger on the

---

* Incidentally, Michigan with its eighteen Electoral College votes also had a Republican governor and GOP control of the state legislature. Michigan is not usually considered a swing state, but Romney's personal ties to the state, where his father once served as governor, were expected to make him competitive. Romney lost by nine points and over 450,000 votes.

problem. "Let's be honest," he says, "you're not running for president—you're running for governor in twelve states, and it just happens to be a presidential election." Statistician and polling analyst Nate Silver—who in 2012 became famous for correctly predicting the outcome of all fifty states—gives an even lower number. "It's only about seven or eight states that can really affect the outcome in a close election, which is the case that people care about."

Walker's framing of the task might sound obvious, but Republicans failed to recognize it, even after the loss in 2008. Ever since Ronald Reagan's landslide victory in the 1980 election, conservatives and Republicans have insisted that America is a conservative nation at its core. This has driven the party to insist on pushing a consistent national message that speaks to conservatives at the level of ideas and values and turns out the party's base by reminding them of the perils of progressivism.

Thus, the problem described in the GOP's 2012 "postmortem"—Republicans have nationalized their election strategy while Democrats have gone hyperlocal. And the results speak for themselves.

In 2004, this nationalized strategy succeeded in giving George W. Bush a second term. But this was more due to the unique nature of that race. Former RNC chair Ed Gillespie explains, "It was really a nationalized election around national security," 2004 being the first presidential election of the post-9/11 world. In that contest, Republicans pushed a "stay the course" message with an incumbent who had already done the groundwork in the 2000 election to win voters' support. A national strategy for a still relatively popular president made some sense, especially when that incumbent was pitted against an unimpressive challenger.

However, open elections like the one in 2008—and the upcoming one in 2016—require both candidates to introduce themselves to a national audience, demonstrate expertise on a wider range of issues than those concerning their previous constituencies, and build a broad base of support. In 2008, Barack Obama did that, running not just a twelve-state campaign for governor, but more of a fifty-state campaign for Congress.

Before that, "no one [in either party] was paying attention to others, only to their base," says Altareit "Pudgy" Miller, a conservative radio host in North Carolina. "So then you got this polarizing guy [Obama] who comes along, and he says, 'I'm going to help you get a job. I'm going to increase these programs. We're going to do it right.'" "James," an official in Miller's county who spoke on condition of anonymity, adds that this engagement produced a nearly unbeatable advantage for Obama four years later, too. "Most people would choose Romney in terms of handling the economy," he says, "but Obama blew him out of the water when it came to which person cares about somebody like me."

"In 2012," says Americans for Prosperity activist Greg Moore, "Romney's campaign was concentrated on TV, TV, TV." That got old quickly. "At some point, there were so many ads to just watch. The people were like, I'm done. Just done. If you're not motivated by something, someone showing up at your door and saying *will you do me a favor and get out and vote* [might work.]"

"Which," Moore adds, "is what the Obama campaign did."

REVERSING THE COURSE

What happened in the states where Republicans used to win elections? That's the question that this book seeks to answer. In order to understand what went wrong in 2012 and begin assessing the GOP's chances for getting it right in 2016, I undertook a project to learn about the communities where Republicans went from winners in 2004 to losers in 2008 and 2012, focusing on one key county in each of seven states that lost Republicans the last two elections.

The choice of states was, needless to say, complicated. A handful were obvious, such as Florida, with its twenty-nine Electoral College votes, and Ohio, a state without which no Republican has won the White House since the two-party era began in 1856. Others were more unlikely. For example, in the last fifty years, Republicans have won Wisconsin only in national landslides, which would normally exclude it from consideration as a swing state. However, Wisconsin's political climate has been transformed in the last decade, and in 2016, its ten Electoral College votes will be within reach for the GOP.

Like states in the country as a whole, each state has counties that are stubbornly Republican or Democrat—but each one also has counties that either party can win. These handfuls of counties serve as bellwethers for the state, demonstrating the reach of national campaigns across the country. And in close elections, these battlegrounds become the difference in delivering their states' votes to the victor.

To assess Republicans' chances of winning in 2016, I have

focused on seven counties that, taken together, hold the key to ninety electoral votes:

- Hillsborough County, Florida
- Hamilton County, Ohio
- Wake County, North Carolina
- Prince William County, Virginia
- Brown County, Wisconsin
- Jefferson County, Colorado
- Hillsborough County, New Hampshire

The data from past elections, from demographics, and from the various economies tell part of the tale of each of these communities—and data play a not-insignificant role in *Going Red*—but it does not tell us about *who these voters are*. So, in order to better understand the concerns of these voters as they look ahead to 2016, I visited all seven of these communities, conducting more than a hundred interviews with activists, elected officials (including one governor and a member of Congress), and regular voters—Republicans, but also independents and Democrats—who wanted to tell their stories. Their insights come directly from those exclusive interviews.

These bellwether counties are made up of different people, different personalities, and different political desires and whims. Even so, many similarities emerged from their recent history and the voices of voters there, and these patterns give an important view of the challenges that Republicans and conservatives face in trying to win back the White House in 2016—and beyond.

A CHANGING ELECTORATE AND A FAILURE TO ENGAGE

In the last decade, significant population shifts have altered the political landscape in most of these counties. In one case, Hamilton County in Ohio, the change has been a massive outflow of people from the city of Cincinnati to its suburbs and then to adjacent counties. For four of the remaining six, the challenge for the GOP is the opposite—growth. But all seven counties have one thing in common: the net effect of population shifts has been to slowly transform a former Republican bastion into a diverse microcosm of the US electorate as a whole. In order to compete and win in these key swing counties, Republicans need to adapt their strategies and messaging accordingly. Their success in doing so will determine their hopes of surviving as a national party in the future.

Considering how the GOP fared in the last two cycles, this isn't as easy as it sounds. In each county, and in every potential demographic within them, activists and voters saw national messaging delivered by people who did not know the turf, and it showed in a lack of enthusiasm among voters.

Ed Gillespie confirms this finding, based on his experience of having worked on the Romney campaign. "I was there in Boston and I worked for Governor Romney," Gillespie says, "and the Romney campaign generally ran the same ads in Virginia that were running in New Hampshire and Iowa and Ohio. To be an effective campaign," he continues, "you really need to be running different ads in Northern Virginia than you are running in Hampton Roads or Southwest Virginia."

To win in 2016, Republicans will need to reconnect to three key constituencies that Barack Obama energized in both of his successful campaigns, each of which will only become more important in the future.

For the past several presidential cycles, Hispanics have been the fastest-growing demographic in the United States, and the GOP has fretted over how to engage them. The most common complaint about Republicans among Hispanic voters is that, even when they get the issues right, their rhetoric precedes them. "Too often," the RNC's Growth and Opportunity Project found, "Republican-elected officials spoke about issues important to the Hispanic community using a tone that undermined the GOP brand within Hispanic communities."

Kelly Maher of Compass Colorado sees an additional problem: Candidates' token efforts to engage her state's Hispanic voters. "They will like hire a brown person with a Hispanic surname. And they will be like look, this is our Hispanic outreach person," which Maher calls "ridiculous," "kind of offensive," and "a giant waste of money."

Hewitt believes the loss in 2012 can largely be explained by Republicans' failure to engage Hispanic voters in general and Spanish-language media in particular. "We got outspent 7:1 on Spanish-language media, which mattered enormously in Florida and Colorado," Hewitt says. "Mitt Romney identified that as his number-one error."

If Republicans failed to engage Hispanic voters on their own terms, they shrugged off African American voters altogether—which has long been a tradition for the GOP. For more than forty years, Republicans have ignored black voters, assuming that they will vote Democratic in overwhelming numbers. This may have been especially true in 2008 and 2012, with Barack Obama at the top of the ticket.

"James" says that the Republican Party doesn't do a good job of even engaging black *Republicans*. "You had presidents of community colleges in North Carolina that are black and Republican. Where are they? Not engaged at all," he says. "North Carolina has the only black chief of staff in the country. When was the last time you've seen him at anything with the RNC or Republican Governors Association?"

That failure hurts the GOP in two ways, the first of which is strategic. Even in 2004,[10] before Obama was on the ticket, African Americans made up 11% of the electorate, and Bush won 11% of their vote on his way to a narrow three-point win over John Kerry. By 2012, the bloc accounted for 13% of the vote, but the GOP only won 7% of it.[11] In close elections, this voting demographic matters, and even a small improvement for Republicans among African American voters can make the difference between victory and defeat.

Beyond the electoral consequences, however, there are moral consequences to a strategy that ignores more than a tenth of American voters. It leaves these communities with no political leverage, stuck between one party that ignores them and another that takes them for granted. "Then, no one has to be held accountable," conservative African American activist Sonnie Johnson says. "Republicans never have to say we're wrong, and Democrats never have to talk about the real evil of the policies they push."

The longer it takes to start engaging, the more difficult it will become to overcome the hurt from what Johnson calls the GOP's "abandonment." And, in the meantime, Democrats will have full reign to demonize Republicans as "this group of people who . . . didn't like certain segments of the population," as D. J. Jordan, vice chair of the Prince William County GOP, puts it.

A third group that has received only fitful attention from the GOP is younger voters. Republicans have committed more resources to engaging with this group than with African American communities—but without much more optimism or real efforts to create a true connection. "The GOP is dying off," says Sara Remini, a Young Republican in Wake County. "If they don't start bringing in younger people . . . the GOP is going straight downhill." When they do arrive, says millennial voter Craig Hunsicker in Jefferson County, younger Republicans find themselves locked out of party positions: "The percentage of white hairs to people that actually have their hair is 90 percent."

Barack Obama took advantage of this gap in both 2008 and 2012. In the 2012 election, the millennial vote accounted for 19% of total turnout, splitting 60/37 for Barack Obama.[12] The Obama campaign relied on a strong turnout among millennial voters, and Republicans cannot count on a low turnout saving them in 2016. Time will literally run out on that strategy soon, if it has not done so already.

Longtime political analyst John Davis sums up the danger of disengagement among all these key demographics for the Republican Party. "Tell me how Republicans are going to win the White House if they don't do a better job reaching out to minorities, young people, urban voters," Davis says, pointing out that the Republicans' traditional base of support is shrinking. "Old-timers, people born before 1946, before the baby boomers, are down to 11.9 percent. That's the greatest generation, the silent generation, [and] so the millennials are now the largest voting age population group in North Carolina. And Republicans don't do well with young people."

If the GOP doesn't make those adjustments, these voters may be saying *What's a Republican?* before long.

DEMOGRAPHICS DON'T NEED TO BE DESTINY

"The central problem for Republicans is that the Democrats' biggest constituencies are growing," wrote Michael D. Shear, the *New York Times*'s White House correspondent, in the wake of the 2012 election.[13] "Republicans increasingly rely on older white voters. And contrary to much conventional wisdom, voters do not necessarily grow more conservative as they age."

Does the changing demographic landscape mean Republicans will soon lose the ability to win in competitive territory? Nate Silver rejects that idea of demography as destiny.

"I tend to think that argument is overrated," Silver says. "Let's assume that parties keep their same share of every coalition, right? Then just the Hispanic population increases, the Asian population increases. Obviously, that helps Democrats," Silver allows, "but it's a pretty slow process." And, Silver adds, "Politics is not static."

Besides, this assumes that neither party will adapt its message to new voters. "If the GOP isn't adapting, then sure, it hurts them," Silver says. However, he adds, "I think Democrats could be in for a surprise if they assume that demographics will save [them]."

Of course, the GOP's effort to adapt has at times met with some resistance. Silver points to the GOP primary campaign in the summer of 2015, with its sharply negative tone toward immigrants and the debate over candidates' use of Spanish on the campaign trail as a potential "step back" for Republicans.

Peter Wehner, a former adviser to George W. Bush, put it in harsher words at the time, writing that "the message being sent to voters is this: the Republican Party is led by people who are profoundly uncomfortable with the changing (and inevitable) demographic nature of our nation."[14] *Led* in this case may be a misnomer; Wehner wrote this about Donald Trump and Ben Carson, whose entire appeal came from their status as outsiders, not as authority figures within the party. But if this view doesn't necessarily reflect the leaders of the party, the more troubling issue is that it *does* reflect a not-insignificant number of its voters, who are worried that appealing to Hispanic, African American, and young voters will require an abandonment of conservative principles.

But adaptation to the realities of changing demographics does not necessarily mean changing the principles of conservatism or the Republican Party, nor should it. If conservatism provides the best outcome for people, then conservatives and Republican candidates should be able to adapt it to improve the lives of *all* people. Sonnie Johnson and Tito Muñoz, conservative activists in the African American and Hispanic communities, certainly believe that conservative principles, especially free-market economics, will better their communities and provide prosperity to the people within them, regardless of their ethnicity or language.

Conservative writer and radio host John Ziegler wrote in September 2015 that conservatives appear to believe that the nation already accepts the conservative agenda and just needs a national reminder of it every four years.[15] "[T]he conservative base is living under several important delusions," Ziegler wrote. "[M]ost of these are in the realm of what kind of a country we actually live in . . . and how easy it will be for a 'real conservative' to beat Hillary Clinton."

On the other hand, the midterm election cycles in 2010 and 2014—with Republicans making large gains in the House and Senate and in state-level gubernatorial and legislative elections—also put paid to the idea that America has become a center-*left* nation. These midterm elections differed from the past two presidential cycles in two key ways. The first will be true in 2016 no matter what: in the midterms, the Obama organization largely sat out of the race. But the second difference gets to the heart of *Going Red*: In the midterms, Republicans succeeded in engaging voters on the ground, especially in state and federal legislative races, instead of simply proclaiming a conservative ideology and expecting voters to adapt themselves to it. In the midterms, the GOP's politics became local once again.

This point is crucial for understanding the seven battleground counties that will decide the 2016 election. In earlier presidential cycles, these bellwether communities conformed more easily to the ideals and outlooks of traditional Republican coalitions, but the large shifts in populations, economies, and demographics have changed them and made them more like the country as a whole. When the opposition is telling people how they can improve their lives and the specific issues within their communities, voters will choose the candidate and party who care for them as they are, not the one who tells them who they *should* be.

AN INFLECTION POINT

Republicans aren't the only party facing a demographic challenge in 2016. In the same story that noted Republicans' reliance on older white voters, the *New York Times*'s Michael Shear also noted that Barack Obama only won in 2012 thanks to the surprisingly resilient turnout machine he built in 2008. "If turnout among blacks, Hispanics, and younger voters—groups that have historically had comparatively low turnout rates—had declined slightly, Mr. Obama might have lost," he wrote. This may present a particularly difficult problem for the next Democratic nominee, as the ground organization that produced two winning outcomes came not from the Democratic National Committee but from the Obama campaign—and it rested on Obama's appeal as a historic and inspirational figure.

Carolina Journal's John Hood very much doubts the same will be true in 2016, even if Hillary Clinton succeeds in her attempt to become the first female major-party nominee. "I doubt very seriously that an eighteen-year-old in 2008, who was a freshman in college, who . . . was excited to vote for the first black president, will in 2016 as a young adult feel the same excitement voting for essentially his grandma," Hood says. "It's just not the same thing."

Open elections—ones without an incumbent on either party's ticket—often serve as inflection points for American politics, as the 2008 cycle proved. Voters not only wanted a change in America's policies, they wanted a serious change in how those policies were pursued. The Obama administration provided both—not in the form of the promised Hope and Change of the 2007–8 Obama cycle, but in the form of a sharply progressive turn in policy, and a much greater exercise of executive power.

In 2016, Republicans will have their chance to offer a change of direction. After eight years of misadventures under the Obama administration, voters in each of the seven battleground communities reported being fed up with the direction of the nation in nearly every policy area. Economics and job creation take precedence in most cases, but also overregulation and continuing issues related to ObamaCare. Foreign policy and national security have gone off the rails, voters in these battleground counties worry, especially with the rise of the Islamic State of Iraq and al-Sham (ISIS) and the retreat of American influence around the world. Mainly, though, they crave leadership that can get things done to address the issues that impact their lives, more than they want another four or eight years of executive triumphalism in service to ideological fidelity. They want *real* change, not just sloganeering for more intrusive big-government solutions.

But in order to take advantage of this opening, conservatives and Republicans must get this election right after failing to do so in 2008 and 2012. If Republicans can't flip these counties and states in 2016, they'll have a lot more difficulty doing so against an incumbent Democrat president in 2020, which means their next chance won't come until 2024. By that time, demographic changes may make the job impossible. The stakes are too high to return to business as usual, or to assume that another national-messaging, base-turnout strategy will carry the day against a less-than-inspirational Democratic opponent.

To win this election, Republicans and conservatives will have to engage voters where they find them, on their own terms, and make conservative policies relevant to their everyday lives. This book is a field guide for that effort in the communities that will decide who wins in 2016. Who are these voters, and what are their concerns? What are the dividing lines between the party, its grassroots base, and the swing voters in these counties? Where are new Republican votes likely to be found? How did the GOP lose these formerly reliable counties in 2008 and 2012, and what will it take to win them—and the White House—back in 2016?

If the GOP can ask and learn the right lessons from these questions—questions that will guide what follows in the rest of this book—they just might have a shot in 2016, and beyond.

FLORIDA

HILLSBOROUGH COUNTY

EVERYTOWN, AMERICA

F or the past sixteen years, the state of Florida has loomed large in Republicans' White House dreams—and nightmares. Republicans have won the state's Electoral College vote in six of the ten post-Watergate presidential elections, but four of the six wins went to Ronald Reagan and George H. W. Bush. By the 2000 election, Florida had become a swing state, widely considered to be crucial for the hopes of both parties.

By that time, a flood of internal migration had made Florida one of the biggest states in the Electoral College, with twenty-five seats up for grabs, or nearly 10% of the total needed for a majority. And of course, in 2000, Florida would remain up for grabs *after* the election, shocking and stunning a nation, and causing Americans to parse the meaning of nomenclature like "butterfly ballots" and "hanging chads" while waiting to find out whether the country would be dragged into a prolonged series of recounts.

By the time the Supreme Court stepped in to put an end to the recount in December 2000, two political realities had become apparent. One, the Republican victory in Florida, and by extension the national election, would remain bitterly contested for many years to come. And two, as the swing state with the largest number of Electoral College votes, Florida would become the center of both parties' White House hopes. In 2016, with Florida's vote total having climbed to twenty-nine, the stakes will only increase.

Even with that history of close contests and demographic changes that have turned Florida purple in presidential elections, Republicans *still* compete well in the Sunshine State. Republicans have won every gubernatorial election since 1998, along with most of the statewide offices. They have controlled both chambers of the state legislature since 1999, and in 2004, George W. Bush took the state easily, beating John Kerry by a split of 52%/47%. The only fly in the Florida ointment has been in the US Senate, which Democrat Bill Nelson managed to win in 2012, thumping former congressman Connie Mack IV by double digits.

But in the last two presidential cycles, Republicans couldn't make the sale. In 2008, Obama won the popular vote nationwide by seven points, but he only carried Florida by less than three. Four years later, with two more Electoral College votes on the line, Obama won only 50.01% of the vote, edging out Romney by just 74,000 in the same race in which Senator Nelson achieved his thirteen-point win. In both elections, Republicans made a better showing in Florida than they did elsewhere, but a loss is still a loss. What happened? How could Republicans do so well in state government elections for the past decade or more, and yet lose two presidential elections by such narrow margins?

The answer lies in a band of counties loosely connected by the Interstate Highway 4. Called the I-4 Corridor, this region cuts an east-west pass through the center of the state, neatly dividing it between the Republican-dominated Panhandle and the Democrat-dominated South Florida counties of Miami-Dade, Broward, and Palm Beach.

"Florida is many states of being in one," says Marc Caputo, *Politico*'s reporter on Florida politics. "The Southeast is the Northeast, and . . . the Southwest is the Midwest thanks to I-75. The North is the Deep South." The Panhandle is a Republican stronghold, reflecting the deep conservatism of the southern states adjacent to it. South Florida, with Miami at its core and the wealthy enclaves on its coasts, reflects the strain of urban progressivism seen in East Coast cities like New York and Boston. "All of these meet in the I-4 Corridor, Caputo explains. "And then you have this band which we call the I-4 corridor . . . that is the mixing zone for all of these different influences."

The I-4 Corridor comprises a number of central Florida counties. Besides Hillsborough and Orange, where Orlando sits at the north, there is also Osceola and Polk to the east and south. The I-4 freeway ends in Hillsborough, but most consider Pinellas to the west to be part of that political parcel, as well as Pasco and Hernando to the north.

In 2008 and 2012, Obama won Florida largely by flipping these counties. Pinellas, home to St. Petersburg, went for George W. Bush in 2004 by a whisper, with a mere 246 votes separating him from Kerry. Obama added 23,000 votes to Kerry's total in 2008 to win the county by eight points. Osceola, a smaller county that has experienced fairly rapid growth in recent years, went for Bush 52.5%/47% in 2004, but swung decisively toward Obama in the following two cycles, giving him 59.4% and 61.73%, respectively.

But the key to the I-4 corridor is Hillsborough County. Bush won it 53%/46.2% in 2004 with 245,576 votes, and McCain came up 9,000 votes below that in 2008, even in a seven-point blowout. But in 2012, Romney actually exceeded Bush's vote total by nearly 5,000 votes . . . and still lost this crucial battleground by nearly seven points.

This result stunned the Romney campaign on election night, and it surprised others who had watched the campaign play out on the ground level. "I'd forgotten it was that much," says *Tampa Bay Times* political editor Adam Smith, who also notes, "Obama did pretty well in North Tampa, which surprised me. I would have thought that was a Republican area." With a margin of exactly 36,000 in the 2012 election, Hillsborough provided Obama with almost half of the margin he got in carrying Florida and capturing its twenty-nine Electoral College votes.

Hillsborough holds the most potential votes that the Republicans can flip in 2016. Miami-Dade has a much higher number of voters—more than 879,000 in 2012—but Bush lost the county in 2004 by over six percentage points, and Romney lost it in 2012 by more than twenty-three points and 208,000 votes. Getting within ten points in Miami-Dade would certainly provide the margin of victory, but Democratic domination in southern Florida makes that a long shot at best. Of the counties that flipped to Obama after 2004, four of them sit on the I-4 corridor, and Hillsborough has the most votes.

But where in Hillsborough did Republicans lose the last two elections? A precinct-by-precinct analysis of lost votes shows two particular epicenters of failure—one of which would surprise most observers.

NEW TAMPA

For decades, cultural critics have complained that the most remarkable feature of American suburbs is their lack of re-markable features, as well as their lack of diversity and their disconnection from the life of the urban centers to which they are attached. Whether or not that generalization fairly represents American suburbs in general, it doesn't take long to discover that it describes New Tampa—the community at the north end of the city, just above the University of South Florida's main campus—to a T. New Tampa provided Barack Obama with some of his largest flips in Hillsborough, and in 2016, this community might just hold the key to a Republican victory.

Other parts of Hillsborough provide plenty of color and culture. Spanish explorers first came to the bay in the early sixteenth century, displacing a Native American culture that went back millennia, but failing to establish anything more permanent than its name. The United States established Fort Brooke in 1824, and despite a total destruction of the town in 1848 after a hurricane-generated tidal wave leveled the village, it rebounded so well that by 1855 it incorporated as a city. Thirty years later, Cuban cigar manufacturer Vicente

Martínez-Ybor moved his operations to Tampa from Key West, and cigars quickly became the city's primary industry.

Today, Tampa prizes its Ybor City historical district, where a handful of local cigar and tobacco stores maintain that tradition. The old brick buildings that once housed the industry now feature nightclubs, restaurants, and a streetcar for tourists to experience it all. The area has added major sports teams to its cultural life, including baseball (Devil Rays), football (Buccaneers), and hockey (Lightning). Add in the beaches and the year-round beautiful weather, and it's not difficult to see why Tampa has become not just a vacation magnet, but a draw for new residents as well.

But for those who end up in New Tampa, color and local flavor are certainly not the draw. The neighborhood developed relatively recently in Hillsborough County. The University of South Florida campus preceded it by a few decades, as did the area around Fletcher Avenue, which is dominated visually by the warehouse-size Todd Couples Superstore, an adult sex emporium, as well as a gun store and local restaurants like Krystal and Wing King of Fletcher. It's a colorful and visually chaotic avenue with plenty of foot traffic, especially as one nears the university campus.

All of this changes once you turn left onto Bruce B. Downs Boulevard, a thoroughfare that serves as the main artery to New Tampa. The street started off as Eight Mile Road, which had nearly no development past the USF campus. Locals referred to it as the "road to nowhere," and a generation of Tampa youth used it for drag racing when their parents and the police weren't watching.

But starting in the early 1990s, development in Tampa exploded, and more than half of the city's growth took place in New Tampa and the surrounding area. The population grew rapidly, rising from 7,000 in 1990 to 26,200 in 2000.[1] By 2010, it had doubled to over 55,000.[2]

However, the growth in New Tampa provided a sharp contrast to trends in the city itself. Instead of open neighborhoods and main streets lined with businesses and shops, gated communities came to dominate the landscape, with names like Portofino, Tampa Palms, Kingshyre, and Heritage Isles. From the street, the only evidence of these communities is their entrances, and as you drive past them on Bruce B. Downs Boulevard, the main drag swells to eight lanes of traffic, ensuring swift commutes through suburbia all the way to the Pasco County line and beyond.

Retail centers dot the side roads of New Tampa but remain somewhat hidden from view of the boulevard. Those who seek them out looking for local or regional flavor will shortly find disappointment. Almost without exception, the colorful fare on Fletcher gets dispensed for the all-too-familiar palette of national chains, such as Panera, TGI Fridays, Ruby Tuesday, and the like. The strip malls look very much like strip malls everywhere else in the United States as well, with bland earth-toned exteriors and standard architecture.

"The people of Tampa will hate me for saying it," Caputo said, paraphrasing Gertrude Stein's lament about Oakland, California, "but there kind of is no *there* there." Caputo meant this about Tampa in general, but one could apply it even more to New Tampa and the walls, gates, and buffer zones of trees that hide the houses and condominiums of the area. But the makeup of New Tampa begins to make sense once one understands how people end up there, and perhaps more important, where they hope to end up.

The privacy of New Tampa's exclusive neighborhoods has attracted an upwardly mobile—and yet diverse—population. In 2010, the median household income level for New Tampa was $73,882,[3] well above Hillsborough County's 2009–13 median of $49,596.[4] The ethnic composition of New Tampa differs significantly from the rest of Hillsborough as well. African Americans comprise 14.5% of the population (down slightly from 17.4% for the county), but Asians account for 11.6% of New Tampa—far higher than the 3.9% in Hillsborough overall. Whites are still a large majority, but at 66.5%, more than nine points lower than the county, at 75.6%.

The key to the puzzle of New Tampa is that the area's growth has been driven by people who are making their way up the corporate ladder; they've moved to New Tampa because of a promotion or change in jobs, and they understand that in order to continue ascending, they will probably need to move somewhere else. This is why the neighborhood has the most generic of retail shops, architecture, and city planning: it creates an all-American suburban cocoon for those transitioning from beginnings to big endings and who don't have the attachment or energy that leads people to engage in their local communities.

In politics, this cocoon is bolstered partly by the fact that most homeowners associations in New Tampa prohibit residents from displaying campaign signs in their yards. "If you put that *My pool is being built by So and So* in your front yard," *Tampa Tribune* reporter Tom Jackson says, "you'll get a note:

Take that down. And the same goes for campaign signs." Jackson has served on association boards and understands the difficulty that associations face in enforcing rules, but he also wonders whether this rule might have a dampening effect on voter enthusiasm and turnout. "It's a sanitizing effect that I think causes us to lose some of our sense of community."

The lack of engagement in New Tampa produces an electoral dynamic that has caught Republicans by surprise over the past several cycles. In midterm cycles, the turnout skews more conservative and Republican, reflecting the political leanings of the more active, longer-term residents. But the upwardly mobile transplants remain engaged in national politics, bringing their perspectives from their communities of origin and changing the turnout dynamics in New Tampa in presidential cycles considerably.

No one knows this better than Shawn Harrison, a Republican who represents New Tampa in State House District 63 and whose fortunes changed when Obama's campaigns brought a new kind of turnout to the polls. Harrison's district dips all the way down to the university and its collar precincts, giving the Democrats an advantage in voter registration. In off-year elections, the turnout model has favored Harrison and Republicans. In 2012, though, Harrison lost his reelection to a Democratic challenger by just 600 votes.

"There was a huge influence from the University of South Florida in the 2012 election that didn't exist in 2010 or 2014," Harrison explains. This effect was particularly acute in 2012 because of the impact Barack Obama had on college-age students. Two of Harrison's current staff were students at USF at the time. "You couldn't walk across campus without hitting at least once by some Organizing for America volunteer trying to get people to register to vote," Harrison says his staffers told him, "and of course they were voting and registering Democrat."

The result, Harrison said, was that voting in the ring precincts around USF in District 63 went up 300% over what it had been in 2010—providing the margin of victory for Harrison's opponent.

Through this defeat, Harrison learned the hard way that he needed to engage with the less affluent voters who live near the University of South Florida campus. "New Tampa has become much more of a melting pot. All different cultures, heritages, races, religions are out here. It's not the typical suburban gated communities that it used to be."

But Harrison's biggest losses in 2012 weren't among minority voters in the ring precincts around USF. They were with the transitory voters—those living in New Tampa on their way to bigger things—who don't engage in state and local politics to the same extent as they do in presidential elections. When they turned out to vote for Barack Obama in 2012, it combined with the heavy turnout in the ring precincts to deliver a coup de grace to Harrison's hopes for reelection.

But for Harrison, the story ends happily. Shortly after losing in 2012, he decided that rather than wait for the turnout model to change, he would seek out voters who usually get overlooked or ignored by Republicans. When he started knocking on doors in the neighborhoods around USF, he was surprised by what he found, and his success provides a helpful example for Republicans and conservatives as they work to flip New Tampa back for the GOP in 2016.

"I had a team of African American supporters who went out into those precincts, and it was amazing," Harrison said. "It was eye-opening." Harrison and his team quickly found that they had misjudged those precincts' priorities.

For instance, the shooting of Trayvon Martin had been fresh in the minds of voters in the lead-up to the 2014 midterms, and they wanted to know Harrison's position on Florida's "Stand Your Ground" law. "They said, 'You can be for it, but here's how it impacts us, here's how we think about this issue.'" Harrison listened to and acknowledged the legitimacy of their concerns, while communicating that he still remained in favor of the law.

Harrison believes this approach of respectful engagement had a profound impact. "When [volunteers] would be out talking to people," he says, "they would say, 'Well, Shawn . . . he's sort of open on some of these issues in a way that you wouldn't think a normal NRA Republican would be open on.' And it helped." Instead of stressing the ideological messaging of the national GOP, Harrison and his team instead talked with residents about what they needed and discussed ways in which he could respond to those needs. His team emphasized that "Shawn is a Republican, but he is a Republican who will be able to help us if we need help."

The results were stunning. "There were precincts that I got 30 percent of the vote in, just north of USF, 99 percent African American precincts. For a Republican to get 30 percent of the vote in those precincts is unheard of. We did it because we didn't try to convert them to the normal old Republican message of pro-family and that sort of thing."

Still, the big flip from Bush to Obama didn't happen in the ring precincts around USF. It happened in the more upscale suburbs in New Tampa, and Harrison thinks that the lack of community engagement hurt there, too. The state Republican Party "provided all the resources I needed," Harrison says, but the local Hillsborough County party "didn't help much at all." Harrison and his team got aggressive in New Tampa.

The first thing Harrison's team found was that the GOP's national messaging was missing the mark. Instead of sounding the philosophical themes of the national GOP, Harrison and his team "identified issues in neighborhoods." The younger generation of voters in New Tampa were pro-life, Harrison found, but they were much more likely to be socially libertarian on issues like same-sex marriage and marijuana legalization.

In Harrison's district, Democrats outnumbered Republicans by seven points, but he won by five and a half points in 2014 to take back his seat. "This is a ground war for me," Harrison says, and Republicans had better prepare for one in 2016 if they want to reverse their losses in New Tampa.

WEST TAMPA AND THE HISPANIC VOTE

If New Tampa lacks local color and flavor, West Tampa has flavor to spare. Where New Tampa's neighborhoods are sealed off from view of the roads, West Tampa's are open for all to see. Local businesses flourish along with the national chains. The La Teresita complex of authentic Cuban cuisine and markets is a required experience for all newcomers, where one can order a delicious—and overwhelming—lunch of *filete salteado,* black beans, and fried plantains.

The enclave was incorporated in 1895 as its own city, across the Hillsborough River from Tampa proper. Thirty years later, the collapse of the cigar industry sent many Cubans from Ybor City to West Tampa, and political instability in Cuba saw many émigrés move to the neighborhoods. Later came waves of Venezuelans, Colombians, and Puerto Ricans, each with their own cultures and political points of view.

West Tampa's electorate has a slight majority of Hispanic voters, but that doesn't quite mean what Republicans and other analysts think, says E. J. Otero, a retired air force colonel who ran for Congress in 2012 in the district that includes West Tampa. "When politicians talk to Hispanics, they are talking to five or six different issues," he says. This becomes an issue, he says, because when Republicans try to work West Tampa before getting to know its people, they start off by talking of immigration reform, and "it doesn't fly."

Otero sees missed opportunities for the GOP in the areas of economics and foreign policy. "If you go to a meeting with an ex-Venezuelan, and you start talking about welfare plan, immigration reform, military, al-Qaeda, they will listen because it's interesting, but that's not [what] makes them tick," he says. "What's going to get them to vote is 'What is your position on the communist regime of Venezuela?'" Puerto Ricans support immigration reform because of solidarity with

Mexican and Central American friends, but the issue doesn't inspire them as much as economic issues, because immigration is a nonissue for someone who's already an American citizen. Colombians, on the other hand, want to hear how candidates will "really put an effort into the free-trade agreement they already have with Colombia."

Jorge Bonilla, who in 2014 ran for a House seat in Florida's 9th District, calls the Puerto Rican communities in the I-4 Corridor "the most important Hispanic vote in all of America—the one that could potentially swing the 2016 election." But Bonilla, whose family comes from Puerto Rico, argues that Republicans need to change their appeal to his community.

"Puerto Ricans have come to Central Florida over the course of the past twenty years looking for economic opportunity," Bonilla says. "But for some odd reason, both national parties up until very recently have hit them with traditional messaging, with immigration messaging that really doesn't apply to them." What would apply to them, he says, is a message that honors the reasons they came to America in the first place.

"Puerto Rico is the ghost of Obama's future," Bonilla explains. "You see the structural debt and everything else that's forcing people to flee the island and how that's crept into some of our cities and some of our states. So there's an opportunity for pickup there, but the Republican Party . . . doesn't know quite what to do with it." Thanks to that failure, and a well-designed ad that exploited Romney's opposition to the nomination of Sonia Sotomayor to the Supreme

Court, the GOP utterly flopped with Florida's Puerto Rican voters in 2012. "Obama carried that group 83/17 in the last presidential election," Bonilla points out.

On economic issues, Otero wonders why Republicans seem reluctant to make a pitch in neighborhoods where their policies would be most needed. "I would go to the homes of very poor people and I would talk to them," Otero said. "There are families out there that actually identify with the Republican message." They want their sons and daughters to get jobs in order to support themselves, and would back candidates who address those issues in practical ways that speak specifically to their community and to their families.

The problem, Otero says, is that Republicans don't bother to get to know either. "The message I hear back," he explains, "is 'Well, you guys don't come to our meetings.'"

Otero became the first Hispanic candidate to win a major-party nomination to Congress in West Tampa. It didn't help Otero much in a heavily Democratic district, but he blames that in large part on Republicans' lack of engagement in Tampa's core neighborhoods. "We live in the same neighborhood. We make the same amount of money. But there is a fence between us and we're not really talking to each other," he says. Republicans don't compete because they don't think the effort will pay off, but that's the problem. "You're not going to go out there as a Republican and have a TV ad and say, 'Vote for me, because I'm a great guy,' and not go to their local meetings in their neighborhoods," he says, echoing Harrison. "It all comes down to the handshake."

Daniel Garza of the LIBRE Initiative, which advocates for

free-market principles in Hispanic communities, points out that Republicans have seen glimmers of hope in their outreach to Hispanic voters. In the 2014 midterms, he says, "you saw this shift now go the other way, favorable to the Republican Party," but it requires candidates who can inspire. "If he's out there, or she's out there, engaging and outreaching, and driving the message that you're going to inspire people on a new model of American leadership," he continues, "Latinos are like other Americans. They're going to be inspired."

Candidates need to understand the context of the communities, and they also need to trust voters there enough to put their arguments in real terms. Garza uses the minimum-wage debate as an example.

"Hillary is out there saying she's going to raise the minimum wage up to fifteen dollars," he says, but the Republican response too often takes the form of attacks on Clinton's character. That turns off voters, Garza argues. "That's not going to get anywhere. It's personal, it's cliché, it gives you nothing, it doesn't tell you anything."

"But if I say, listen, the truth is if the minimum wage goes up to fifteen dollars an hour, do you know who is going to get laid off?" Garza asks. "You know whose businesses are going to close? My uncle Jesús Corona, his business is going to close. He's barely on the margin right now. He's barely making it, and if you put that thing up to fifteen dollars an hour, forget it," Garza answers. "And the rich people, the guys who have the big stores? All they're going to do is jack up the prices, and so guess who has to pay higher prices? We do."

"If you tell that narrative," Garza concludes, "you're

saying, 'Hillary doesn't care about you,' and that's going to make a difference."

In 2004, George W. Bush managed to win key precincts in West Tampa on his way to winning Hillsborough County. The Republicans' fates changed in 2008, when Barack Obama emerged as a transformational candidate, but Otero argues that neither party learned any lessons from it. A "high-ranking Democrat" told Otero that "the Democratic Party takes [West Tampa] for granted, and the Republican Party ignores us." Otero notes that the stimulus package pushed by Obama allocated $42 million to Tampa, but hardly any of it got spent on intended goals—fixing the streets and infrastructure in the struggling neighborhoods there. In fact, Otero found out that only $15,000 got spent in heavily African American East Tampa.

Otero tried campaigning on that lack of competence and poor constituent services but struggled to overcome the harm done by the GOP's national messaging. In 2012, Republicans ran against the stimulus package, but it was already a fait accompli. They should have focused on its distribution, or lack thereof in these cases, as evidence that Democrats take poor voters for granted. "If you go to the African American neighborhoods, they're destroyed," Otero says. "You go to some of the Hispanic neighborhoods, they're not much better than they were thirty years ago. And the Republican party is not seizing that," missing a prime opportunity to make inroads into traditional Democratic Party turf.

In order to succeed there, though, Republicans must offer a positive agenda for the future, and not just argue the negatives of the Democrats—especially since so many voters there identify as Democrats. Otero recently arranged for a Republican candidate to address a meeting of voters in West Tampa as a means to build support for conservative economic policies. The candidate's message of competent governance, reduced red tape, and economic empowerment began to inspire the crowd, Otero says . . . right up to the moment when the candidate shifted to the attack and began lashing out at Democrats. Otero watched the crowd's reactions, seeing plainly that they had rejected not just the messenger but also the message. One angry audience member told Otero that when the candidate was trashing Democrats, "He was talking about *us*."

The *Tampa Bay Times*'s Smith agrees, and says that the Republicans fundamentally failed by trying to convince people in these areas to "fire Obama" rather than elect Romney. With the economy bouncing back in Tampa, "people were feeling a little bit better about things here," and Romney did not offer a good reason to vote for him. "It was mostly trying to make the case that they shouldn't vote for Obama," and it ended up turning off voters who might otherwise have been open to an authentic Republican message.

Scott Terry agrees with Otero and Smith on this point. A Tampa native, Terry moved into an economically reemerging neighborhood called Tampa Heights after growing up in the wealthy and conservative South Tampa area. His new neighborhood has only recently reversed a decades-long decline, with people "rehabbing old bungalows" and opening restaurants in dormant retail areas. "It's gentrifying," Terry says about his community, a process that has created controversy for more than a decade,[5] but which has produced "arguably the most diverse neighborhood in the city."

Perhaps not for long, though. "More and more, the residents are white," wrote Ron Matus, Denise Watson Batts, and Cathy Wos for *City Times* in June 2004. "Lured by sweet deals and city-backed loans, hundreds of urban pioneers refurbished Victorian mansions, chased away drug dealers, and cleaned up trashy lots." The remaining residents from the days of African American dominance in the neighborhood feel pressure to move out, while incoming residents tend to turn neighborhoods like Tampa Heights into "upper-middle-class enclaves," observed Urban Land Institute senior fellow John McIlwain in the article.

Democratic politics dominate Tampa Heights for the moment, and unlike the precincts in New Tampa and West Tampa, Tampa Heights pulled for the Democrats in all three of the last presidential cycles. The new influx of people and money offers Republicans an opportunity to gain a new foothold in Tampa proper, but the party has yet to calculate a message that inspires voters in this area. In fact, Terry believes that the strident anti-Obama messaging in 2012 did more damage than good.

Republicans missed the implications of the dynamics that Obama's candidacy created. Obama and his campaign generated a deep emotional connection, especially with younger voters who saw themselves as the vanguard of a new kind of politics. Terry recounts a visit to neighbors who had a Barack Obama bumper sticker—on the refrigerator. In talking with the couple about politics, he was surprised to find that his neighbors seemed open to conservative ideas, especially their policy ideas. The connection to Obama was one of core identity. "They just feel like, 'Oh my gosh, we're younger people, we need to vote for Obama.'"

Attacks on Obama in 2012 missed that point, and instead sounded to these voters like an attack on their own judgment. "A lot of people who voted for [Obama in 2008] didn't want to feel like fools," Terry says, adding that the swing voters Republicans sought in 2012 had chosen Obama in 2008 for a change from the old political patterns. Obama had an emotional connection to these voters, which was based on making them feel better about themselves for joining his movement. To them, negative attack ads against Obama felt like an attack on themselves for their choice in 2008.

From Terry's perspective, Obama's retirement from politics creates an opportunity in Tampa Heights—not necessarily to win the neighborhood, but certainly to become more competitive. "Obama was the embodiment of the 'I don't want to be one of these old people who's against everything'" dynamic in Tampa, especially among younger, upwardly mobile urban voters, Terry explained. "I don't know that another candidate will be able to tap into that," he continued. "I don't know that Hillary Clinton is going to have that same pull and attraction for a lot of voters."

Republicans need to focus on building "positive, forward-looking messaging" rather than attacking Democrats, Terry said, echoing Otero. "One of the big issues is opportunity. This isn't a big social-issue town." The mayor of Tampa, a Democrat, has worked to bring new opportunities and jobs to the city and has garnered the respect of voters in the areas where Republicans hope to compete. This kind of pragmatic politics works better than ideological combat, especially in places where Republicans tend to be outnumbered anyway.

"It's easier to do that on the local level, of course," Terry allows, but Republicans didn't seem to put much effort into it at all in 2012. "I didn't get that feel from Romney" or his team, Terry says. The emphasis on social issues hurt efforts to reach out to potential swing voters in Tampa Heights as well.

A better strategy would be to run on competence—"that we're going to do a better job, we have plans to improve the economy"—but to personalize it by knowing the voters. The winning message would be "We're *going to make a difference in your life* by improving the economy, we're going to increase jobs *in your neighborhood*" with Republican economic policies. "That is the type of message that could potentially sway voters in this neighborhood, and some of the swing voters in the more traditional Democratic areas."

Those approaches are the antithesis of the "47 percent" ideological messaging that Republicans used with their base in 2012. They are messages of inclusion—and will only work if Republicans get on the ground and make these arguments face-to-face with these voters.

GOING RED IN THE SUNSHINE STATE

No one needs to wonder why Republicans must win Florida in order to win the presidency. Democrats have other big states on the coasts with large numbers of electors—primarily New York and California—but Republicans do not have as many big-ticket states on which they can rely. Without Florida, a GOP victory becomes all but impossible.

To win Florida, the Republican nominee needs to win the I-4 Corridor, and most observers agree that Hillsborough provides the best indicators for statewide outcomes. "Marketers have known about Hillsborough's ability to predict outcomes for products, even for years," Jackson said. "So if your message sells in Hillsborough, there's a pretty good chance that it's going to sell in Orange and Volusia," and most of the I-4 Corridor.

By now, with the population growth in South Florida, the Republican nominee may need to score big in Hillsborough and other I-4 Corridor counties in order to win the state. "There's a little whisper of this in the last election that maybe Florida wasn't as much of a swing state as people made it out to be," local activist and political blogger Peter Schorsch says. He points out that Jeb Bush won Miami-Dade County in 2002, but that was "with the advantage [in Miami-Dade] only Democrat +1. What happens when it's Democrat +14?"

To reverse the Democrats' advantage, the campaign will have to work big. First, they will need to limit the margin of losses in Miami-Dade and Broward Counties, both largely Democratic in presidential elections. Next, they will need a superior "get out the vote" (GOTV) effort in Northern Florida, the traditional Republican stronghold. But, most important, in order to compete for Florida, Republicans must pull off a convincing win in the center ground of the I-4 Corridor.

A win in Hillsborough would prove that a Republican candidate has been able to reach outside the base and speak to a diverse populace with a message of hope. This may be especially true within the growing population of Puerto Rican voters, whose numbers may increase significantly for 2016 owing to the municipal bankruptcy in the territory in 2015. That crisis in San Juan may provide an opening for Republicans to offer a commonsense set of economic and fiscal policies, and Hillsborough's population of transient voters will test whether they can transform that into a winning message across demographic lines in other states, too. Even if the nominee can't win every demographic, if the campaign can make a more competitive position than Romney or McCain, it may make all the difference in this narrowly fought state.

OHIO

HAMILTON COUNTY

ANCHOR OF THE BUCKEYE STATE

F ew political realities are as enduringly true as the Republican Party's need to carry Ohio in presidential elections. The next time a Republican nominee wins the White House while losing Ohio will be the *first* time it has ever happened in the era of the two-party system. Since 1856, there have been forty presidential elections, and Ohio has only chosen the losing party five times (and all five were in support of Republican candidates).[1] But that support hasn't carried over to the post-Watergate area. In every election since 1976, the GOP has lost its iron grip on Ohio, and the state has become a bellwether for the national result.

Thanks to the decline in the Buckeye State's percentage of the US population, Ohio has lost electors in every census and reapportionment since 1970. Currently, it has eighteen Electoral College votes, two-thirds of what it had at its peak, but both parties still see Ohio as a must-win state. And for any candidate hoping to win Ohio, the must-win area is Hamilton County, which anchors the southwest corner of the state and includes the metropolitan area of Cincinnati.

Traditionally, Hamilton County has been a Republican bulwark. Until 2008, Lyndon Johnson was the last Democratic presidential candidate to win Hamilton County.[2] Even in years when the rest of Ohio voted for Jimmy Carter (1976) and Bill Clinton (1992 and 1996), Hamilton remained stubbornly Republican. "Hamilton County was more Republican than Ohio or the nation in every single presidential election from 1932 until 2004," notes Kyle Kondik, managing editor of *Sabato's Crystal Ball* and author of an upcoming book on Ohio. "And we're not just talking about slightly. It's usually in the high single digits or higher, sometimes getting over ten points."

In 2004, George Bush narrowly won Ohio by two percentage points and 118,000 votes.[3] Had John Kerry won the state's twenty electors, he would have been president. The election was so close that Senator Barbara Boxer attempted to prevent Ohio's electors from being seated for the official Electoral College vote,[4] but the Senate refused to play along with her ploy. Hamilton gave Bush a boost of almost 23,000 votes alone and a 53.25%/47.1% edge, helping to ensure his victory.

Four years later,[5] Republicans' long winning streak in Hamilton came to an end when Barack Obama beat John McCain in Ohio by nearly five points, more than doubling Bush's margin of victory in 2004. For the first time in eighty years, the Democratic candidate's margin in Hamilton was wider than in Ohio as a whole—by 53%/46% and almost 30,000 votes. That was a flip of 53,000 votes in just four years, demonstrating that population shifts alone did not account for the loss.

In 2012,[6] Mitt Romney expressed confidence that he could carry Ohio against Obama, but that confidence was misplaced—and in Hamilton, the results got worse. Obama won the state by just a shade under three points, 50.58%/47.6%, and 166,000 votes. Once again, however, Hamilton turned even bluer than the state, giving Obama more than 20% of his statewide margin of victory. Romney failed to outpoll McCain, coming up more than 2,000 votes short of the Republican total in 2008.

In the eight years between 2004 and 2012, the overall vote total in Hamilton decreased by 6,000, but Democrats picked up 30,000 votes, while Republicans *lost* almost the same amount. What happened?

QUEEN CITY AND HER COURT

According to local lore, the city of Cincinnati sits on seven hills* as it hugs the bank of the Ohio River and overlooks neighboring Kentucky to the south. A historical allusion to the other city of seven hills—Rome—also gives Hamilton County's largest city its name. Lucius Quinctius Cincinnatus was a leading statesman in the early Republic who was twice given dictatorial powers in order to keep the Romans safe. Both times, he resigned his dictatorship promptly at the end of the crises, choosing not to keep power for a day longer

---

* The city of seven hills is actually a piece of civic mythology. The *Cincinnati Enquirer* noted in 2008 that there were more than seven hills in the city, but the paper also acknowledged that it had helped perpetuate the myth fifty years earlier. "City of Seven Hills," *Cincinnati Enquirer,* December 4, 2008, http://archive.cincinnati.com/article/99999999/CINCI/81202017/City-seven-hills.

than necessary, even though he might easily have become a grand ruler. Instead, Cincinnatus chose in both instances to return to his farm.

Cincinnatus's example of service and humility made him a legend, and when George Washington declined to rule the newly declared United States as a military dictator despite his massive popularity, his contemporaries proclaimed him a "modern Cincinnatus."[7] A statue of Washington as Cincinnatus sculpted in 1791 by Jean-Antoine Houdon explicitly cast Washington in that role, depicting him in civilian clothes standing behind a plow, as Cincinnatus is classically portrayed. It stands in the rotunda of the Virginia Capitol in Richmond to this day.[8]

The city's other nickname—the "Queen City"—hints at more noble aspirations. In 1819, Ed Cooke wrote in the local newspapers that "the City is, indeed, justly styled the fair Queen of the West: distinguished for order, enterprise, public spirit, and liberality, she stands the wonder of an admiring world." The nickname "Queen City" stuck, so much so that Henry Wadsworth Longfellow immortalized it in his poem, "Catawba Wine."[9]

The modern Cincinnati, however, more resembles the modest example of its namesake, as well as the other former manufacturing powerhouses throughout the Rust Belt that hit hard times when the US economy went global. Over the last few decades, the city and county have made attempts to transition to a more modern service- and technology-oriented economy, but Cincinnati's manufacturing base tenaciously holds on.

"We have a lot of Fortune 500 presence here," says Jeff

Capell, a Hamilton County voter for the past sixteen years. "There is a big GE plant, the Kroger headquarters is here, the Procter & Gamble headquarters is here, Macy's head-quarters is here," Capell continues. "You definitely have a lot of corporate white-collar jobs here, but since it's Ohio, there is naturally a good amount of manufacturing here as well."

Like many Rust Belt cities and counties, Hamilton and Cincinnati have seen a decline in population—the only county among the seven highlighted in this book to have a net exodus. The outflow from Cincinnati, in particular, has been dramatic and ongoing for more than a half century, going from a half-million people in 1950 to 298,165 today. In three of the five decades since 1960, the population has declined by more than 10%.[10] Cincinnati has experienced some growth in the last four years, according to the Census Bureau's 2014 estimate, but only by a rate of 0.4%.[11]

Some of the city's residents have migrated to other parts of Hamilton County, while others have left altogether. Unlike Cincinnati, Hamilton's population grew in the 1950s (by 19.4%) and the 1960s (6.9%), but it began a decline after that—with a 5.5% drop in the 1970s, the worst decade. Now estimated to have 806,631 residents, Hamilton's population remains 12% lower than its peak at 924,018 in the 1970 census.

This sharp drop in population has changed the dynamics of Hamilton County politics. "You have more affluent white Republicans leaving the county," says one local Republican Party official, "in favor of suburban communities that fall outside [Hamilton]. There are a lot of great Hamilton County Republicans living in Butler, Warren, and Clermont."

Thanks to the relative ease of access to Cincinnati, even those who still work in Hamilton have little problem commuting from these surrounding counties.

Those who had less income and mobility but still wanted to move out of the urban center ended up in working-class neighborhoods just outside the city, making these communities more diverse, more working-class, and more Democratic. And it was in these first-ring communities of Cincinnati that Democrats saw their largest gains between 2004 and 2008 and 2012.

Migration doesn't account for all of the change, however. George Bush won those communities in 2004 on his way to a narrow win over John Kerry in Ohio. A combination of Barack Obama's inspirational candidacy and the GOP's abandonment of the strategies that used to bring success in Hamilton County produced one of the most shocking reversals in 2008—and in 2012.

FIFTY-TWO PICKUP

Part of the challenge in addressing Hamilton County and Cincinnati is the distinct, tight-knit communities that form both. Hamilton, besides Cincinnati, has forty-eight local governments with which residents most closely identify, and the city of Cincinnati contains fifty-two separate and distinct communities, neighborhoods defined by their high schools and their churches. And, to some extent, their chili.

Travelers who come to Cincinnati may find themselves confused when first encountering the city's chili culture.

Queen City chili bears only a passing resemblance to the familiar Tex-Mex dish chili con carne, instead reflecting Cincinnati's unique heritage. This chili comes from Macedonian immigrants to the area in the 1920s,[12] two brothers named Tom and John Kiradjieff, who created a stew that includes spices like cinnamon, cloves, allspice, and now occasionally chocolate to put atop hot dogs, called "coneys" in Cincinnati.*

One does not order a bowl of chili in Cincinnati, as this author discovered firsthand at Price Hill Chili in West Price Hill. Cincinnati chili does not come as a dish on its own, but in combinations, or "ways," as locals order it. A typical two-way would have chili atop a bowl of spaghetti, with succeeding layers built onto it. A "five-way" consists of pasta, chili, beans, onions, and a mass of shredded cheese.

One's choice of chili serves as an identity marker in Hamilton County. When asked to name his favorite chili place, Ed Bell laughs and says, "That is very divisive. It's like the Ohio State–Michigan [rivalry]." His wife, Gena, quickly proclaims, "I'm a Skyline girl!" Ed finally admits, "I prefer Gold Star," and then jokes, "even though that kind of paints me as someone who doesn't appreciate fine cuisine."

Price Hill Chili serves as a central political gathering space for the Price Hill neighborhood, represented in the state legislature for three terms by Lou Terhar. Terhar, after

---

* In almost a century since the Kiradjieff brothers slapped their chili onto coneys for the first time, over 250 chili parlors have sprung up in the city and county, and the chili industry generates more than $100 million in annual sales.

instructing me in the "ways" of eating chili in Cincinnati, explains that these neighborhoods stick together. "I won four of the nine wards in Price Hill, because my signs were purple and white. That's the high school colors," Terhar explains. "No one who didn't go to that high school would have the courage to put that sign up in this town."

Jeff Cooper, a local voter, confirms Terhar's observation about the importance of high school alma maters. "People ask, where did you go to school? They don't mean college," he says.

Church membership provides yet another form of local identity, and one that sticks. "There's a lot of Catholics, and then there's the Greek Orthodox Church," Cooper says. "They have their festivals. Everyone goes to that." Cooper grew up in Oakley, a neighborhood on Cincinnati's East Side, but moved out several years ago. No matter: "We don't live in Oakley anymore, but still go to the Oakley church festival."

To win this election, says "Mike," a conservative activist who prefers to remain unnamed, it will take knowledge and understanding of these layers of community. "We have fifty-two neighborhoods," Mike says, "and they all have their own characteristics and really unique demographics." To win Hamilton County, and in turn Ohio, you need to know the differences and connections between them.

WEST AND EAST SIDE STORY

Given the population exodus and the hard economic times for Rust Belt cities like Cincinnati, it's no surprise that some neighborhoods have struggled. Some, like Lower Price Hill, have declined into abject poverty. Others, like Over-the-Rhine, have gentrified in the last fifteen to twenty years, a matter of no small controversy in Hamilton.

A study by the Federal Reserve Bank of Cleveland of housing values for the last seven years before the 2008 financial crash showed a handful of previously declining neighborhoods like Mount Airy and the Heights undergoing renewal. Critics of gentrification blamed the increase in rent and housing prices for forcing longtime residents to move north in search of lower costs of living. In December 2013, Randy Simes wrote for *UrbanCincy* that Cincinnati was gentrifying at the fourth-fastest rate in the Midwest, "only behind Chicago, Minneapolis, and St. Louis."[13]

Part of this issue has to do with long-standing cultural differences between the east and west sides of Cincinnati, and of Hamilton County in general. "You've got to know the lay of the land," says Zac Haines, a businessman active in Republican Party politics in Hamilton. "Hamilton County, it's very different because you have the city, but then here, there's an east side and a west side." The east side has a white-collar, upper-class connotation, while the west side has a "stigma" of working-class neighborhoods.

The cultural split plays across the entire county, John O'Leary says, although it is no longer as pronounced as it was, even just a couple of decades ago. "My aunt grew up on the east side, and she complained that all of the west side people were angry, because they had to drive to work with the sun in their eyes and they had to drive home from work with the sun in their eyes," he recalls.

The split even went to sports team identity. "The west side was always Reds. Everyone likes the Reds, but baseball is in their blood," O'Leary says. "The east side is the Bengals crowd, traditionally. Reggie Williams described us [eastsiders] as the wine-and-cheese-eating crowd. It's definitely changed, so it's not so defining, but if you go up against Western Hills kids in baseball, you'll get your clock cleaned."

All of this points to a key issue in Hamilton County, which is having the knowledge to successfully navigate the culture and politics of communities that think in radically different ways. In 2008 and in 2012, Republican presidential campaigns failed to pull this off—and paid the price for their failure.

LITTLE PINK BALLOTS

To some extent, as in other areas of the county, the candidate made the biggest difference, especially in 2008. "Barack Obama ran to the center. He made a lot of promises, and Hope and Change are very appealing," Haines says. "You have a guy who is very inspiring and you have the prospect of the first African American president. That is appealing in and of itself. . . . He talked about transparency. He talked about things that I think everybody can agree with."

Nathan Nickell, vice chair for the Young Republicans' Southwest Ohio chapter, chalks some of this up to Democratic unity and Republican disunity. "It's because while the Democrats united behind Barack Obama, they may not have agreed [on every position]," he explains. Nevertheless, they pulled together during the election. "They're like, 'of course I'm going to vote for him. He's the Democrat. I'm not going to agree with the Republican more.' You don't see that with Republicans around here."

Almost everyone agrees, however, that the Obama campaign simply outclassed the McCain and Romney campaigns. "The Obama machine turned out votes that we've not seen turned out before," says county commissioner Greg Hartmann, "particularly amongst the city neighborhoods. African American vote turned out higher than ever before and delivered over 90 percent of that vote to Obama. We saw crowds for early voting that we have never seen before."

Besides, as Gena Bell recalls, the GOP didn't even bother to show up. When she worked as a poll judge in the 2008 election, "we didn't have one Republican person at that poll handing out the pink ballot. Maybe they are not going to take it," Bell says, and "the likelihood that they are all going to vote Republican is probably very slim, but we [were] not even there engaging the people. You need to show up."

North College Hill city councilman Ron Mosby—an African American conservative—agrees. "You had a number of Republicans that didn't come out to vote. Period." Mosby also feels as though other voters weren't inspired enough to make a change. "The last three presidents we've seen have won two consecutive terms," he points out. "Now are you going to tell me that every president did such a great job that they deserve reelection? Or was it easier for the voters to simply say, 'I'll just maintain status quo'?"

The Obama team put its resources into a superior get-out-the-vote effort, Lou Terhar says. "They drove folks. They had black churches packing buses going to the polls Sunday after church, because we're open on weekends," Terhar notes about early voting. "They were lining up to vote like crazy."

Republicans did a much poorer job at GOTV, especially in 2012, when the Romney campaign's ORCA computer system for GOTV ended up as a spectacular failure. "Numerous Republicans in and around the Romney campaign called the ORCA platform a total bust," *Politico* reported days after the election,[14] "stranding thousands of volunteers without a way of reporting data back to headquarters and leaving Romney central command without a clear view of developments on the ground."

Republicans on the ground in Hamilton grit their teeth to this day when you ask them about 2012. Haines certainly remembers it, calling the ORCA system "an absolute disaster." The secrecy of the rollout and the lack of sufficient real-time testing became rapidly apparent on Election Day. "People didn't know how to use it. It was just an absolute mess," Haines says. "So the technology, the tools and equipment we were using—it wasn't a level playing field."

Bernie Daniel, who has worked every election since 1952, switching from Democrats to the GOP after the Carter presidency, said that Republicans' woes in 2012 started with bad data collection.

"Republicans have this habit of hiring college kids to run what they call victory stations," Daniel says. "I'm not sure those kids are very committed to the cause. They're just trying to churn up numbers. Because that's how they get paid."

The canvassers were supposed to do passes through neighborhoods to find undecided and lightly committed voters for the final GOTV push. "If they say, 'I'm for Romney' or 'I'm for Obama,' you cross the list committed. You should never come back to that house, because you don't waste time going to the house of committed voters," Daniel says. "I was sent to the same house at least three times, so these kids who are working these campaign victory centers—as they call them here in the Ohio Republican Party—are obviously not doing their job."

Maggie Cook, a local conservative activist and veteran of many election campaigns, puts 2012 succinctly. "In 2012, the ground game just sucked. There is no other word for it."

Have Republicans addressed this glaring disparity in the time since 2012? Cook believes that local activists have begun to fill the gap. "Our party leadership is working very hard on it, here in Hamilton County," she says, noting several surprising local successes culminating with the 2012 defeat of incumbent Republican congresswoman Jean Schmidt in Ohio's newly redrawn 2nd Congressional District. Podiatrist Brad Wenstrup shocked Schmidt in the primary with a 49%/43% win, and went on to handily win the district in the general election, 59%/41%. Wenstrup won the 2nd Congressional District's Hamilton County precincts with 59% of the vote at the same time that Obama won it from Romney.

"Even judicial candidates, city council candidates, county and township commissioners, and trustees are [now] very aware of their ground game," Cook says. "They are doing a lot of work, and that is where they are spending their time and their effort." Most of those precincts fall in Hamilton's east side, and the demographics and economics of those precincts are much easier for Republicans.

Hartmann agrees that the GOP has done "much better" to improve the infrastructure, calling the difference "night and day," and praising RNC chair Reince Priebus for making critical reforms in the Republican Party and restoring the confidence of its major donors. "Some of the sophisticated donors aren't just going to give money for the RNC to fly first class," Hartmann quips. "They want to pay for something that is going to turn vote out and identify voters. I think that we are far more sophisticated than we were before. A lot of that didn't get recognized, I think. But that kind of infrastructure gives us the kind of traction we need to win an election."

It had better, because the demographics paint a bleak picture for Republicans as they seek to reclaim Hamilton as their anchor in southwest Ohio.

THE DEMOGRAPHIC WRITE-OFF

While the exodus from the Queen City, and to a lesser degree Hamilton County, doesn't account for the huge flips in voting over such a short period of time, there is little doubt that the demographics of the remaining population of Hamilton present a huge challenge to the Republican Party. In fact, one could argue that it's the most difficult environment for conservatives and Republicans among the seven counties featured in *Going Red*, providing the clearest test of whether the GOP can expand its reach when Barack Obama leaves the political stage.

Ohio as a whole closely resembles the United States in several key aspects. It tends to be slightly more Caucasian than the United States, 83.2% to 77.7%, and African Americans make up a slightly smaller part of the population, 12.5% to 13.2% nationally.[15] In Hamilton, however, the picture shifts dramatically. Black residents account for 26% of the population, double the national average, while the percentage of white voters drops to 69.2%. In Cincinnati proper, the two populations come almost into parity—49.3% white, 44.8% black.[16]

In contrast, the Hispanic population remains much smaller on both the state and county level. Hispanics only make up 3.4% of Ohio residents and 2.8% of Hamilton and Cincinnati residents as well. The Asian population is even smaller, at 1.9% in Ohio, 2.3% in Hamilton, and 1.8% in Cincinnati. In age and income demographics, though, Hamilton looks more like the rest of Ohio. Its median household income slightly exceeds the state's, but both fall more than $4,000 below the national median. Hamilton's poverty rate (18.7%) is significantly higher than Ohio's (16.0%) and the national rate (14.5%), mainly because Cincinnati's poverty rate is 30.4%.

How can the Republican presidential campaign reach voters in such a diverse environment, especially after having lost an eighty-year advantage in Hamilton? Councilman Mosby says Republicans first need to learn that they must fight for votes here. "At one point, Hamilton County was taken for granted," Mosby says, "and I don't think you can say that anymore."

There is a flip side to this lesson, too. Too often, Mosby says, Republicans use data to write off large portions of the population, missing their chance to keep up with changing demographics. Mosby's community gave Bush a 97-vote edge in 2004, but flipped more than 1,100 votes to Obama in 2008 and over 1,500 votes in 2012. Mosby says he earned respect from voters for visiting supposedly lost-cause precincts in a losing effort for a seat in the state legislature. If the GOP refuses to break out of safe zones, it will become a self-fulfilling prophecy, Mosby says. "People are going to say, 'You didn't care about me anyways, so why should I vote for you?'"

Voters want an emotional connection to a candidate, Mosby says, a sense of the real person rather than the persona painted by their opposition. "If you go out and you talk to them—talk *with* them, not talk at them—they're going to remember that when it comes time to vote. They may not vote for you, but they can't get out of their mind, oh yeah, this person came to visit me. That, I think, is the key."

Arnold Kalti has lived in Hamilton for all fifty-nine years of his life, the son of Romanian immigrants. The ethnic makeup of the county has changed considerably from when he first bought his grandmother's house in Western Hills. "At that time, when I was living out there, it was German immigrants, middle class," Kalti recalls. "And if you were to go there today, you would not recognize the neighborhood. It's changed that dramatically. The houses have deteriorated. The income levels have gone down dramatically."

Kalti argues, though, that Republicans have made a mistake by shying away from these neighborhoods. "It's not so much to try to talk to them, it's just to reach out to them," the lifelong conservative voter says. "Just to say hey, we understand. Here's our position, and go talk to them." Kalti has done so, and finds that they want to hear from Republicans, even if they may not necessarily agree with them. "I asked them flat out," Kalti says, and these neighbors told him, "We've voted Democrat almost all our entire lives, and that's because nobody ever reaches out to us. This is all we know."

This cycle gives Republicans an opening to engage these communities, Hamilton County GOP chair Alex Triantafilou says, and he believes that the GOP has to use this cycle to start opening those doors. In fact, Governor John Kasich has already done so. In 2014,[17] Kasich ran against Democrat Ed FitzGerald, winning reelection by more than thirty points and taking all but two counties (Monroe and Athens). Kasich carried Hamilton by almost twenty-five points and 56,000 votes, just two years after Obama won the county by more than 26,000,* and he even achieved victory in the Democratic bastion of Cuyahoga.

"John Kasich did particularly well among African American voters,"† Triantafilou says, even considering the nature of the landslide win. "I want to say he got 25 percent to 26 percent of the African American vote, which is unprecedented."

This did not happen by accident, Triantafilou argues. He

---

* It's worth noting that Ed FitzGerald's candidacy was widely considered a disaster, apart from Kasich's strategy and GOTV efforts.
† Triantafilou had a good memory. According to NBC's exit polling for the Ohio gubernatorial race, Kasich won 26% of the African American vote statewide.

credits the RNC with pushing for engagement. "There has absolutely been a focus here in Ohio on the African American outreach program. There is a fellow here in Cincinnati named Jeff Pastor who is an African American, hugely dynamic, awesome, hardworking guy," he says. "When he starts talking, every conservative in the room just falls in love with him, because he's saying all the stuff that conservatives believe. . . . So Jeff has been on the ground here for a couple years as a full-time paid staffer of the GOP."

"A window is about to open for Republicans on this," Triantafilou predicts, when asked about 2016. "We have the opportunity [to engage] without embarrassing President Obama, because he'll be forever wildly popular among African American voters. We do have a window to say, let's try another way. Let's try another way to lift everybody up. Let's try another way to help in job creation."

"Mike" feels the effort has been long overdue, and that Republicans' absence from these communities gave Democrats the opening to define the GOP in harsh terms. "The longer that we take to really show up at their doorstep and tell them how Republican policies can really fix their communities, the more the Democrats get to paint us as whatever they'd like," the activist says. Republicans have to acknowledge that the experiences of these communities are different from those in suburban Hamilton or in the Over-the-Rhine and Hyde Park neighborhoods. "We need to recognize that disparity that exists—and the Democrats have been recognizing it and talking about it for years. And just because we recognize it doesn't mean that we're the cause of the issue or that we're on their side or the folks on Wall Street. I think it means that it makes us look aware. And," Mike adds, "maybe it gives us a foot in the door."

SINKING THE PUTT

Once the foot is in the door, how do Republicans make the sale in all the different and disparate communities in Hamilton? Mosby wants Republicans to start with a unifying vision that can speak more broadly than the old partisan lines. He points to the days when Republicans stood for abolition, liberty, and the Civil Rights Act. "The point is that it was bigger than the party itself."

The one issue that Mosby believes could unify voters in Hamilton County is education, a subject of deep concern across all demographics. Mosby has experienced the transformational power of education in his own family—and it's likely that many readers may have been touched by it.

His father, Frederick Mosby, was drafted into the United States Navy during World War II. After the war, the elder Mosby studied mechanical engineering at the University of Rochester, graduating with a bachelor's degree and a commission in the US Naval Reserve. Four years later, Frederick went to work for General Electric and in 1955 set to work to develop an alternative bulb for automobile headlights that used incandescent lighting exclusively. Mosby patented the first practical A-line halogen lamp, although it would take another decade for it to start appearing in cars.[18] Most vehicles now on the road rely on halogen lamps of the kind Mosby's father developed, thanks to the investment he made in his education.

"Education is the one area where that has been neglected for so long that it's actually larger than the people or the party," says Mosby, who sees this as a liberty concern that transcends other divisions. "We're not teaching, we're not telling the students how to think, we're telling them *what* to think," he emphasizes. "That literally transcends the party."

Debe Terhar couldn't agree more. She served as president of the Ohio State Board of Education for four years before her husband, Lou, ran for the state legislature, and sees education as a priority, especially in struggling Cincinnati.

"I fought for four years to try to get year-round schooling in," Debe says. The "summer slide" creates problems for many children, especially in economically stressed families, and eliminating it would improve retention as well as avoid weeks of remedial review. "As a teacher, it used to take me six weeks to get kids caught up between September and October to the level they were in June when they left. It's just ridiculous."

In working-class neighborhoods on the west side of Cincinnati, education is a quality-of-life issue that hits home with voters. "Their concerns," Lou says, "are, Is my kid going to get an education? What's going on with my property tax? And can you keep my neighborhood safe?"

The Terhars aren't as sure about the issue of education transcending political divisions, however. "She had a job where she could never be right," Lou recalls. "She got attacked right and left for the same thing at the same time. You can't be right in education." Still, in a culture where the high school alma mater provides an integral part of one's identity, education issues will play an important part on Election Day at every level.

For other voters, the economy takes precedence. John O'Leary, a Republican from the solidly middle-class Blue Ash community, says the downturn hurt many in Hamilton, and some have still not yet recovered from the blow. "Since 2008, I'd say half my friends have either lost their jobs or had to transition at some point," O'Leary says, believing that this also drove the results in 2008 and 2012. Most of those "have caught on since," but "that was a big problem, people just losing their jobs."

Included now in the economic concerns are the unexpected impacts of ObamaCare. "I just got dinged on it," O'Leary says. "My company has tried to keep our premiums so that we wouldn't have [an] increase for the past fifteen years, and then [they] went up 27 percent with the Obama-Care, and starting this year they said we can't keep the policy, otherwise they're going to charge. Our $300 family deductible went to a $3,000 family deductible."

Republicans also need to frame economics as an issue of liberty and regulations, Debe Terhar says, especially on ObamaCare. "Look at what they did with [it]," Debe says, "the number of hours you can work. Full time is no longer forty hours, and now it's twenty-nine hours. What happens to those eleven hours that you've now lost pay for? How are you supposed to pay your rent? How are you supposed to feed your kids? How are you supposed to pay for your insurance?" The issue, Debe says, should be framed by Republicans as "freedom from the regulations that are holding people back from starting new businesses or being able to add to their businesses."

Jason Cooper, a young voter who manages a major-chain retail store in Hamilton County, says the economic issues go deeper than just how many jobs have been created or lost, especially among millennials. "Six or seven years ago, we had 1,400 hours per week for the store," Cooper explains. "It's one of the [chain's] larger stores. Now we have *maybe* 800 hours, and we're expected to do the same amount of work. That's just a small thing, but you can see there is a lot less money in employment, but they're making the same amount of money in the revenue."

Miguel Dilbert has a different perspective about millennials. Talking over a bowl of ice cream at Graeter's, a Cincinnati chain of specialty parlors, the biracial millennial sees the problem as too much demand for "free stuff." That's especially true when discussing the most pressing economic issue for voters in his age group, student debt. Rather than go to college, he got a well-paying job with a major shipping company and now makes more than most of his friends who attended universities.

"Unfortunately, the vast majority think that if they get the degree, they should just be handed the fat check and just show up to work," Miguel says. "Clock in, clock out, and make $80,000 a year, just because I got a bachelor's degree on the wall. But the problem is they end up finding out those jobs don't exist. Now they have all of the student debt. They're moving back in with their parents. Maybe they found a decent job. Maybe they found a mediocre job. But it's always less than they expected, and now they are frustrated because they are paying more in student debt than I'm paying on my mortgage."

This disillusionment feeds the progressive-populist momentum on the Left, Miguel says, and it frustrates him to see it. "Bernie Sanders is their knight in shining armor, saying you should be forgiven" your debt, Miguel says, and that makes it difficult to argue for reality. "Because then there are people like me who literally are sweating every day, and I make a good living. But I earn every penny I make. And you want to take more of my pennies? Because why?"

Republicans need to tap this reality, Miguel advises, although he admits it's no easy task, as he discovered when debating the fifteen dollars per hour minimum wage with a friend. "He was like, 'Man, that would be great.' I was like, 'That's a horrible idea.' He was like, 'Why?' And I just broke it down for him." Miguel explained the inflationary impact on wages and how the change would result in little change in buying power, but in layman's terms rather than in economic technical language. "I put it as simply as I can. I'm like, dude, that dollar burger isn't going to cost a dollar anymore."

Lou Terhar believes that if the GOP could learn to cut through misconceptions in the way Miguel advises, they would win Hamilton outright. "If a Republican can articulate all the things that were done in the last six years that have hurt the average American and his ability to have a job that pays enough to have a lifestyle that is legitimate, I think that guy wins the prize."

Mostly, though, Hamilton County voters want someone who gets things done. "People are pretty pragmatic down here," Lou says. "Tell me something is going to work. Don't give me all of this [ideological] stuff. What's going to work? How do you attack the problem? Give me something I understand. I want to understand how that is going to affect my family."

Commissioner Hartmann agrees. "We've still got a tremendous amount of challenges in this country, and I think problem solver is going to carry the day," he says. "Democrats won because they projected more of an ability to focus on the economy that affects their lives. That's going to again determine the next presidential election in the next cycle—who can do the best job at being a problem solver and fixing a lot of these problems."

Competence and pragmatism will attract people to the Republican candidate, says Zac Haines. "Say let's make government more efficient and more effective," he advises, but "then you have to go a step further. Why are we doing these [policies]? Make sure people who need help get it quicker, better, and faster," Haines answers. "And so we don't have to raise taxes and have jobs, and good companies who provide jobs don't leave our state or go upstate. That's the extra step. We don't go the extra step. We've got to finish off the answer."

As Triantafilou puts it, "If we could just *sink the putt.*"

GOING RED IN THE QUEEN CITY

For at least the last fifty years, Ohio has been a true bellwether state for presidential elections. No Republican presidential nominee can win without Ohio, and Democrats face a tricky path to victory when Republicans hold it.

Mathematically, this may not seem so cut and dried, especially with the decline in Ohio's electors over the last fifty years. Politically, though, the failure to carry Ohio demonstrates a lack of connection to working-class voters, in the Rust Belt and beyond. John McCain lost Indiana in 2008, another state normally considered a Republican favorite in presidential elections, and Barack Obama showed that the old Reagan Democrat coalition of working-class Rust Belt voters had become vulnerable to splintering in presidential elections, if not in midterms. But with Obama retiring, the GOP no longer needs to attack the emotional connection he had with these voters, and Republicans have a window of opportunity to make a new case for their brand of leadership.

After two straight shocking losses in Hamilton, Republicans should understand that they need to reconnect with voters and demonstrate that they have recovered in what should be a GOP stronghold. But a loss in Hamilton would almost certainly doom Republicans in Ohio, and with it, their hopes of winning back the White House.

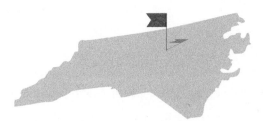

NORTH CAROLINA

WAKE COUNTY

SMARTSVILLE, USA

The 2012 election didn't produce many high points for Republicans. Two of those high points were Indiana and North Carolina—states the GOP won back from Obama—but even those meager gains didn't say much about Republicans' long-term prospects. Indiana had clearly reverted to its Republican traditions, and North Carolina had taken an extreme amount of effort—and barely flipped back in the end. If Republicans don't identify and learn from what went wrong in 2008 and 2012, North Carolina may not stay Republican for very long.

Even starting in the 2012 primaries, neither Romney nor Obama managed to inspire much passion in the state. By the time of the Tar Heel State's primaries in May, Romney had already wrapped up the nomination, and Obama ran unopposed in his. Nevertheless, Romney only won 65.6% of the vote in the Republican primary, with both Ron Paul and Rick Santorum scoring double-digit percentages—even though Santorum had officially withdrawn from the race by that point. Almost 51,000 North Carolina Republicans went to the polls to mark "No Preference," accounting for more than 5% of the vote.

Obama didn't do much better. No Democrat had challenged Obama in his bid for renomination, not even a stunt candidate for a particular cause, even though some grumblings had already begun to emerge from the progressive caucus about a lack of commitment from Obama to their agenda. Not surprisingly for an uncontested primary, Democratic turnout fell short of the Republican showing,[1] but more than 200,000 Democrats showed up to vote "No Preference" for an unopposed incumbent president of their own party.

But this lack of enthusiasm in North Carolina didn't stop the two campaigns from pouring cash into the state. According to a *Washington Post* analysis,[2] the only states with larger ad buys were Virginia and Ohio. Romney outspent Obama $57 million to $40 million—even though the media markets in North Carolina charge lower rates than the markets in the top three states. Nationally, both campaigns engaged heavily in negative advertising—85% of all advertising for Obama was negative, according to the *Washington Post,* and 91% of that for Romney.

Unlike in some other states, turnout actually increased in North Carolina from 2008 to 2012—and, unlike in other high-turnout states, the voters' enthusiasm didn't translate into good news for Obama. In 2008, Obama had won North Carolina by less than 15,000 out of 4.31 million votes. Four years later, North Carolina cast 4.5 million votes in the presidential race, but the difference went mainly to the Republicans; Romney won almost 142,000 more votes than McCain had in the previous race, while Obama only added about 36,000 votes.

These gains helped Romney to win the state, but that

doesn't mean his showing was impressive. Obama's win in 2008 was only the second Democratic victory in the state since southerner Lyndon Johnson won in 1964—the only other being fellow southerner Jimmy Carter in 1976. Prior to the 2008 election, Republican presidential candidates considered North Carolina relatively safe territory, even when outmatched in the rest of the country. Bob Dole beat Bill Clinton in 1996 by 111,000 votes, and George W. Bush won 56% of the vote in North Carolina in both of his presidential elections.

What happened to the Republican edge in North Carolina?

THE PIT AND THE PARTISAN PENDULUM

Wake County sits near the geographic center of North Carolina, and it also serves as the state's center for culture and, maybe even more important, barbecue. Like many southern states, North Carolina gets serious about its barbecue, but unlike some states, it has two distinct schools of barbecue—eastern and western—which differ on both the sauces and the cuts of pork used. Downtown Raleigh is where the two converge, making it possible for one to enjoy a fine eastern-style meal of whole hog and vinegar-based sauce, or choicer cuts with a tomato-vinegar blend in the western style.

Wake County predates the founding of the United States. Settlers first began farming and forming small communities in the area in the 1730s, and they formed the county in 1771 by consolidating three smaller units. In 1792, shortly after the conclusion of the American Revolution, the county seat became the capital of the new state and was renamed Raleigh after the explorer Sir Walter Raleigh, a sponsor of the original Roanoke Colony.

Even in Wake County's early days, growth came from outside migration and investment. First came the railroads, and later, universities and technology. The Research Triangle Park area will look new to visitors, but it began in the 1950s as a concerted effort to leverage North Carolina's standard of living to attract tomorrow's technology. Nestled between three major universities—the University of North Carolina at Chapel Hill, North Carolina State University, and Duke University—this hub of world-class companies and organizations continues to drive population growth in Wake County.

Carolina Journal's John Hood calls Wake County "a microcosm," noting that it is "full of people who are from somewhere else." Some come to Wake County for better employment opportunities, especially if they work in Research Triangle Park, but many are graduates from the area's universities, who choose to stay in North Carolina for the low taxes and comfortable lifestyle.

Regardless of how or why people came to Wake, come they did—and in droves. The population of Wake County grew 44.4% between the 2000 and 2010 censuses,[3] making it the fastest-growing metropolitan area in the country. Since 2010, Wake County has grown another 10.8%, placing it in the top fifty fastest-growing counties of that period[4] and finally pushing Wake's population above one million residents in 2015.

Wake's ethnic makeup looks similar to that of North

Carolina as a whole. Some key differences do emerge, though, especially when you look at the education level of Wake residents. Of the adults in Wake County, 48% have a bachelor's degree or higher, compared with 27.3% in the state, and high school graduates comprise 91.6% of adults (compared with 84.9% at the state level).[5] Wake's population is also significantly younger than the rest of the state, with only 9.7% of its population over sixty-five years of age (as compared with 14.3% in the rest of the state).

The county doesn't get its share of retirees, not even the so-called half-backers. (Hood explains the term: "They move to Florida, and then they move halfway back up.") A number of factors come into play for such retirees, such as the desire for closer connections to family back home, and especially lower taxes, but most of the half-backers settle farther west. That leaves the influx of voters into Wake even more disproportionately younger and less likely to reflect the more conservative history of the state.

Voting patterns in the past three presidential elections reflect Wake's dynamic growth and the influx of voters who are younger and less likely to have conservative roots. In 2004, George W. Bush won 50.8% of the 348,844 votes cast. In 2008, Barack Obama won 56.7% of 442,245 votes in Wake, and in 2012, he got nearly 55% of 486,427 votes. The electorate had grown by 39.4% over the preceding eight years, and by almost 10% between 2008 and 2012—even while the number of votes cast nationally declined by 2.8%.

The migration of newer Wake residents corresponds to the precincts Republicans lost in the last three presidential cycles. People looking to establish themselves and start their economic progression come to first-ring suburbs like New Hope, Wilders Grove, Knightdale, and Brookhaven—looking to get the feel of an exurb and avoid the higher taxes and costs of living in the city, yet still keeping in reach of everything Raleigh has to offer.

Like many Wake County residents, Mitch Kokai came here to attend the University of North Carolina and stuck around after graduation. A local broadcaster and journalist, Kokai has been part of the Wake County political scene since the late 1990s and has watched the population explode since that period, mostly from college students who stayed as he did and younger workers coming for well-paying jobs. This shift has changed the county's party affiliation, and even the character of the people there who *do* identify as conservative. "You've got a lot of people who moved in who may or may not be Republican," Kokai says, "but even if they are Republican, they might be northeastern Republicans," more moderate in temperament.

CARING AND CHARACTER

Hood cautions that the usual blasts against government will fail to make an impact for Republicans in these areas. Voters in Wake County don't want to dismantle public services; they want them to run more efficiently and responsibly. "They don't see government *in particular* as objectionable," Hood says, even if they do "see government *in general* as objectionable." The newer middle-class voters in Wake want less of an ideological argument and more of a pragmatic program based on competence and accountability.

John Davis, who has covered North Carolina politics since the Ford administration and boasts a 96% prediction rate in almost 1,400 elections at all levels over the past forty years, puts the issue more bluntly. Republicans, Davis said, completely missed the economic crisis that voters felt over the past two presidential cycles and insisted on talking about what North Carolina voters felt were irrelevancies.

"It's almost like your house is on fire," Davis says. "Republicans come as first responders and they knock on your door. They say, 'We see your house is on fire. Yeah, you've got kids in there. Okay, well, before we deal with this house fire, I'm going to talk to you about same-sex marriage.' And you're thinking, Oh *shit*." In 2012, the GOP insisted on discussing controversial moral issues at a time when people were desperate for help. "The perception was that Republicans cared more about principles" than voters, and the results showed.

Republicans must add *caring* to *character,* Davis argues. "The first time I realized the importance of caring as a character trait was Bob Dole and Bill Clinton in '96. ABC did a poll asking who has the greatest strength of character. Bob Dole wins 2:1. Who cares more about people like you? Bill Clinton wins 2:1. Next critical question: What's more important, character or caring? Caring wins 2:1."

That, Davis argues, was what sustained Clinton through the impeachment. "The more smut the special prosecutor dumps on Clinton, [the more] his numbers go up. Finally after the bills of impeachment were passed in December of

1998, his positive approval was higher than Ronald Reagan's ever was," Davis recalls. "How in the world is this possible? Don't they see the man is cheating on his wife and lying about it? [. . .] But character is also about caring. Caring is also a character word. And that's the problem with Republicans. Republicans have this list of character attributes that doesn't include caring. But caring is character, and until they add caring to their character list, they're going to stay in trouble [with] the American public."

In order to attract voters living through economic transition in either direction, Republicans need to recognize the generational character of Wake County voters but take the correct lessons from the differences—the first of which is that those differences don't always hold. "Just because someone dropped acid in 1967," Hood says, "doesn't mean they're a Democrat forever." Ronald Reagan did better among younger voters than Republicans traditionally do, and his legacy had more staying power as a result. Hood worries that the Obama generation may show the same effect. "Voting for Obama—will that be like the Generation Xers voting for Reagan or liking Reagan when they were twelve? That's the question," Hood says.

Structurally, Republicans may have at least one change working in their favor. In late 2013, the North Carolina legislature enacted a series of voting reforms,[6] including a change to the ballot order and especially the elimination of straight-ticket voting. Until then, North Carolina had been one of just a handful of states that provided voters with a single check box that would automatically allow them to endorse all the candidates of one party on the ballot.

In 2012, the majority of voters in the state used straight-ticket voting, with 300,000 more Democrats than Republicans taking advantage of it.*

Andrea Dillon, a local conservative activist and writer, believes the elimination of straight-ticket voting may have an impact on turnout, as will other reforms that passed, including the elimination of "preregistration" for sixteen-year-old students. Most of those youths registered in school, and for the Democratic Party. Without that preregistration as part of schoolwork (many students went through registration to earn credit in civics classes, according to the *Washington Post*'s Reid Wilson), the youth vote may indeed drop, at least somewhat. But even before those reforms were made, Republicans had made significant gains at the state and local level.

Dillon thinks this reflects organizational struggles within the Democratic Party. "The Democratic Party here is an absolute train wreck of a mess," she says. "I've got a lot of my Democrat friends who have made comments along the lines of, 'My Democrat Party is in my father's Oldsmobile.'" The leftward drift of Democrats nationwide and in the state, and the increasingly "screechy" quality of the party's rhetoric makes her friends "uncomfortable," Dillon explains, and many of them are reregistering as unaffiliated. "Or," Dillon says they decide, "I think we'll stay home."

Republicans may feel tempted to rely on Democratic

---

* Obama lost North Carolina in 2012 before the reforms that eliminated straight-ticket voting or preregistration.

ennui and organizational woes in 2016 as an easy path to victory. But this would leave them at the mercy of Democrats, who will almost certainly spend time and money in North Carolina—and specifically in Wake—to reclaim the state. If Republicans hope to prevail, they need to not just reach out to new voters, but also reconnect with those who have left the GOP—many of whom live in the town of Cary.

CARRYING CARY

Before the creation of the Research Triangle in the 1950s, Cary had been a small town to the west of Raleigh, founded in 1750 as the Bradford's Ordinary settlement. As in the rest of Wake County, the railroad began to bring people to Cary a century later, at about the same time as farmer and railroad agent Allison Francis "Frank" Page renamed the town after an Ohio congressman and temperance activist he admired, Samuel Fenton Cary.[7]

Real growth didn't immediately follow the railroad or Page's rechristening of the town. By 1960, the population of Cary had reached only 3,356—more than double that of the previous census, but still very much a small town. But the arrival of the technology business changed everything. By the 1980s, Cary had grown by a factor of almost seven, and the growth was only beginning. The 2000 census put Cary's population at 94,536, a 115% increase over that of 1990, and in 2010, its population hit 135,234. The Census Bureau estimate for Cary in 2013 put it just over the 150,000-person mark, a growth rate of 11.7% in just three years.[8] Today, Cary is the seventh-largest city in North Carolina, and one of its most prosperous.*

Cary provides one of the anchors to the Research Triangle Park area, sometimes called "Smartsville, USA." "Cary would be more of a place where the family moves," Kokai says, "after you've got the kids, and you don't want to live downtown anymore and [need] a place for these kids to run around."

This influx of residents has changed the dynamic in Cary, which previously was marked by a brand of Republicanism that emphasized social issues. For new voters in Cary, who are investing in first homes and looking to increase their economic standing, fiscal issues far outstrip social ones—and the latter can turn off voters that Republicans' economic vision might ordinarily attract. These voters want to hear "a positive vision for the future . . . focusing more on jobs and boosting the economy."

"Sixty-six people arrive every day in this county," says GOP activist Zan Bunn, "forty-four by relocation and twenty-two by birth." The influx of people, many from northern and more liberal states, helped the Democratic Party sweep the county commissioner elections in 2014, a rare local bright

---

* The median household income in Cary is $90,250, almost double that of North Carolina as a whole. Per capita income is much higher in Cary, too—$41,554 as opposed to $25,284 statewide. The median value of owner-occupied housing units is $303,700, again almost double the North Carolina average of $153,600. The technological growth of the Triangle has given Cary a substantial tax base for its municipal activities.

spot for a party whose standings in local and state elections have hit their lowest ebb since the 1920s. And Bunn says this will make Cary, and Wake County, tough sledding for Republicans in 2016.

Despite all its growth, Cary puts a lot of effort into keeping its small-town identity intact. Its downtown area harks back to an era of small-town Americana. Local businesses and retail stores line Chatham Street. On Academy Street, historic homes sit beneath the spreading trees on the road, and at the south end of Academy, restaurants like Belle at the Jones House, where a former farmhouse becomes a venue for elegant dining, stand out as links to Cary's small-town past.

These contrasts between past and future put considerable political pressure on the present, and no one understands that better than Don Frantz.

Frantz owns a car repair business on Chatham Street, serves on the town council, and on weekends races his own car at Wake County Speedway. Thanks to his position on the town council and his wife's volunteer service at their children's school, the Frantzes lead a busy civic life. They work together at the shop, which is where these parents of six (most of whom have left the house) spend much of their time together. "If I didn't work with my wife," he explains, "I wouldn't see her."

Until 2015, Frantz affiliated himself with the Republican Party, winning elections to the Cary town council on multiple occasions. Frantz even went to the 2008 Republican Convention in Minneapolis as a delegate for North Carolina. "I've sat in a room and made phone calls for eight hours a day,"

Frantz recalls. "Went around with folks knocking on doors. Anything that I could do to advance conservative governance is what I tried to do."

But in 2015, Frantz went back to being unaffiliated.

"I just grew disenchanted with the party," he explains. As a conservative with "some libertarian leanings," he grew frustrated with the party's "obsession with the social issues." "If it doesn't cost me money or doesn't negatively impact me or my family," Frantz says, "I don't care. I really don't. It's always baffled me how the party of individual responsibility, freedom, and limited government are the first ones to insert themselves into somebody else's bedroom or up a woman's skirt."

Frantz wanted more focus on economic policy, but when North Carolina's Republicans took power, the "first thing they focused on was ban[ning] gay marriage." People in Cary found this "disheartening," Frantz says. After that, Republicans worked on redistricting instead of pursuing an agenda to "fix the economy, grow jobs, tax reform, those kinds of things."

Frantz also sees a tendency among Republicans to make "everything a litmus test. If you don't conform to these ten ideals, then you're not a real Republican." After ten years in and out of office, Frantz had had enough of the GOP's increasingly shrinking tent, and he warns that the litmus-test approach turns off more people in Cary than just himself. "They try to impose their will and ideology on [people] without explaining why," he says. People in Cary want to have their problems addressed "with ideas and solutions, not rhetoric."

In 2016, Frantz says, it's important that conservatives get

over the last eight years and concentrate on the future. "I don't like Obama. I haven't liked him for eight years. I got it," he says. "You guys don't like him either? All right. Move on." After eight years of Obama, voters in Cary and Wake County "want to hear a positive agenda," Frantz says. "They don't want to hear any more about why Obama sucks or why the country is going into a ditch. Tell us how to avoid it."

Frantz still sees reason for optimism in Cary, but Zan Bunn, who works to organize local voters for the GOP, is less hopeful. The 2014 state and national elections initially had Cary voters thrilled with the change in power, she reports—but it didn't last long.

"I know a ton of people were actually disappointed with the way the Speaker vote went," Bunn says about John Boehner's reelection to his position in the House of Representatives in January 2015, emphasizing that she has "nothing against" the Speaker. "A lot of people saw that as a test," she explains. "If you are a state representative and go to Washington and vote again for the same leadership, are you going to do anything different on the budget? Are you going to do anything different on homeland security? Are you going to do anything different on anything?" Bunn shrugs. After that vote, Bunn says, people stopped responding to her organizing efforts. "One after the other, people said, 'So sorry, I'm done with the Republican Party.'"

Bunn says that Cary Republicans aren't seeing much help from the state and national party. Just north on Academy Street from where we met, a local festival was taking place. "I wonder if we're represented," Bunn muses. "We're probably not." When asked if she believes that Democrats had engaged more often and more effectively at cultural events such as this, she replies, "I do."

In one sense, Bunn allows, this may be a product of the broad victories the GOP has enjoyed in North Carolina, including Romney's narrow win in 2012. The GOP managed to end "a 140-year Democratic monopoly" on state government, which may have made Republicans too complacent. "Maybe people think we don't have to do that because we didn't have to do all of those things in order to win the supermajorities in the North Carolina House or the North Carolina Senate and the governor's race."

The major hurdle Bunn sees, however, is simple demographics. Two-thirds of growth in Wake County comes from emigration, not native birth, and even though these voters were attracted by the lower cost of living, Bunn says this is a two-edged sword for Republicans' low-tax messaging. "You run into people from New Jersey, New York, the Northeast all the time, who are coming here. . . . They think this tax burden is low, and they can perhaps tolerate [tax increases]."

Bunn disagrees with Frantz to a certain degree on GOP support for social conservatism and the policy positions, but she agrees with him on the need to stress the positive power of the individual. "Young, old, black, white, male, female," Bunn wants to hear, "if there is a culture of welcome for business, starting businesses, growing businesses, reduce tax burdens, and that can help you as an individual grow an idea that you have into something that gives you a secure future for your family. When was the last time you heard someone stand up and explain that? In simple, optimistic, positive terms?"

YOUNG (AND RESTLESS) REPUBLICANS

Wake County has an active Young Republicans chapter, which by coincidence happened to have a meeting on the day I arrived in Raleigh. By the time I got there in the early evening, the side room at Tyler's Restaurant & Taproom had already become a lively hive of conversation, growing louder as more and more younger voters and activists arrived. Conversations spilled out onto the otherwise unused patio area, part of a sidewalk shared with other businesses in the multiuse complex at Seaboard Station. The featured speakers included state party officials, a candidate for chair, and a hastily arranged speaking slot for myself after blogger and activist Markeece Young introduced me to the emcee.

Before and after my address, which mainly focused on national political trends and a desire to know more about North Carolina, several young Republicans shared their views on the direction of the party—and they're not altogether pleased with it. Markeece Young, a soft-spoken and thoughtful African American conservative, wonders why Republicans allow the media and Democrats to define them rather than engaging voters to define themselves. As a result, voters "think we're for the rich people, we're all white . . . but we're not all white," Young emphasizes. "We're not all rich. We're just trying to do what's best for our country."

At the same time, Young wants Republicans to focus less on Democrats and more on their own positive agenda, especially on economic opportunity. "We're the premier people for having economic opportunity, but we don't address that," he says, especially when it comes to communicating their agenda to black voters. "We always say . . . get off of the plantation or get off of this or get off of that. Get off the Kool-Aid, and stuff like that," Young says. "That doesn't work."

Christian Greavey, a transplant from Massachusetts, agrees that Republicans have to ramp up engagement and have the conversations that can change minds, especially generational voting patterns that favor Democrats. "How do you break through that? You break through that by having conversations with people."

The larger problem Greavey sees, though, is that younger voters have a libertarian streak—and that they see Republicans as no better than Democrats when it comes to telling people how to live their lives. "What we see from folks from DC is, whether they're Republican or they're Democrat, they're telling people how to live their lives," he says. "Where I think we can be most effective, is we tell people, 'Hey, make your own decisions. Give yourself some sort of safety net—we don't want anyone to go cold, hungry, or whatever—but we're not going to tell you how to live your life.'"

Democrats awoke to the power and potential of millennial voters in 2008, Greavey points out, but Republicans have yet to grasp it. A camera malfunction during the interview gave Greavey a chance to needle me on this point. "See, you're an old guy," he said, laughing. "You've got a camera. You should be just busting out your phone."

More seriously, Greavey observed, "Our voters tend to be dying off, and we need to find some way to resonate with folks our age." The problem goes beyond ideology, to some extent; "it's just new folks versus old folks." However, ideology plays an important part in the generational barrier. The party establishment favors the older figures, but "the energy is with the young, the more libertarian movement" at all levels, Greavey says. Republicans seem "openly hostile" to libertarians, and he predicts that this will create "some issues" in 2016 and beyond. If the establishment at least offered some respect and access for libertarians, Greavey predicts that Republicans "would never lose an election. And all you've got to do is play fair."

Another young activist, Sara Remini, echoed Greavey's sentiments. Remini also identifies as "more libertarian leaning," but she sees a little more openness to the libertarian approach than Greavey does. "They've been pretty welcoming," she feels, adding that the old guard has compromised and tried to accommodate the younger libertarians, mainly out of necessity. "The GOP is dying off," Remini says, so if they can't attract and retain younger voters, they are "going straight downhill." It is a matter of numbers, and of survival.

Ted Cruz had an event in April 2015 in Wake, and his approach impressed Kokai. "He really spent almost no time on social issues, did not talk about immigration," Kokai notes. "He spent his time blasting ObamaCare and talking about boosting the economy. He tailored his message for our audience very well." Kokai believes all other Republicans will need to do likewise in order to impress younger voters in the first-ring and technology corridor suburbs.

Dillon sees opportunity in the grassroots conservolibertarian groups, which keep springing up of their own volition. "The average citizen is getting more active," she says. "I've seen a proliferation of American liberty clubs, freedom clubs, this kind of club, that kind of club. We're seeing a more active voting populace out there actually trying to make a difference," Dillon concludes. "They feel more engaged. They feel more *connected*."

WAKING UP TO THE NEW WAKE COUNTY

Perhaps no group of voters in Wake County feels more *disconnected* than its African American community. More than one in five voters in North Carolina and in Wake are African American—yet Republicans routinely concede this demographic, and Democrats take it for granted. Only recently have the state and local party apparatuses begun to realize its potential, and the danger of writing it off. Presidential campaigns have routinely remained disconnected—or worse, treated black voters almost as a scientific curiosity.

This has frustrated Altareit "Pudgy" Miller, a community activist in North Carolina and the president of the Loving Fathers Society, a group dedicated to bolstering families in the community. In 2008, Miller voted for Obama, expecting a change to a newer, fresher kind of politics. Miller, who today is a conservative, also found himself dazzled by the glamour of the Hope and Change message—and the glamour of those who helped deliver it.

"In 2008, back when I was on the Obama train," Miller recalled, "we went to New York City, and they [had] a room full of celebrities there." The event was for Rock the Vote, which had no official connection to the Obama campaign, but the celebrities showed up for a very clear reason. "You know what they were talking about," Miller says.

Republicans didn't have many celebrities in 2008 or in 2012 to speak to the black community . . . or anyone else, either. Miller recalls the effort that the Obama campaign team put into cultivating voters in Raleigh. "They were here in North Carolina a year before the election started. An entire year," he emphasizes. "They spent money in the community."

Republicans, on the other hand, did very little with black voters, and what they did was largely ineffective; as Davis noted, Miller says Republicans talked about their own agenda without getting to know voters or learn their needs. Miller agrees with Davis on the misfire from what little outreach came from the GOP. "Make sure you say hello to somebody before you start talking about your agenda or your values or what may have you," he advises. "Hello goes a long way, man. It opens the door to endless possibilities."

A Wake County official involved in the black community, whom we'll call "James," emphasized the same point. Some of the problem was simply structural, he said, with Organizing for America (OFA) simply outclassing Republicans and conservatives both technologically and culturally, both in 2008 and in 2012. "They got Beyoncé and Jay Z, and we have Clint Eastwood," James said about the difficulties in competing culturally. Even apart from that, the mechanisms of outreach were ill conceived and poorly run. "We were still pulling horses and buggies, while they were driving around in . . . a Bugatti."

The RNC recognized this disadvantage in its "autopsy"

after the loss in 2012. RNC chair Reince Priebus pledged to conduct better outreach into minority communities to build lines of communication and trust. The GOP has committed serious resources to this project, but black conservatives in Raleigh give skeptical looks when asked about it. James at first would only shrug and say "no comment" but later elaborated on what he thought about the outreach. "It was sold to the public different than it actually is," he said, having seen the training for it in Wake County. "It's about data collection," and not making a personal connection.

Data collection is necessary, he acknowledges, but without real, personal engagement, it becomes almost an anthropological exercise, which will almost certainly send the opposite message that Republicans want. *Hello goes a long way, man.*

James offered an anecdote about how engagement offers surprising opportunities. While waiting in line to pay at a cafeteria, the woman ahead of him didn't have any cash, and her bill was below the minimum for using a credit card. He paid her bill instead. "She turned around and asked me who I am and who I work for, so I told her," he recalls. "Just because of that kind of act, she's going to support my boss for reelection."

Republicans have an opening here, James argues, because the 2008 and 2012 efforts by Organizing for America were separate from the Democratic Party. It was OFA out in the community, he recalls, "building the relationships with the people," not the Democratic Party. Before OFA, Miller says, "it was ACORN [Association of Community Organizations for Reform Now] . . . paying people based on how many [people] they registered to vote," while at the same time providing services to those in need within those communities.

OFA has shifted its focus to advocating for Obama's agenda, but the free-market grassroots group Americans for Prosperity (AFP) has filled the gap on the Right since the 2012 election. "Instead of those two brothers [David and Charles Koch] saying they were going to spend $900 million . . . on radio air," he explained, "they set up these permanent offices in these different states." They offer outreach training to volunteers, but they also serve the communities in which they operate, a point that OFA learned but which both parties have ignored. "They're putting them in homeless shelters . . . teach[ing] the homeless about the basics of fiscal responsibility and teach[ing] them the understanding of the Constitution." The latter point has practical use for people on the margins of society, and who want to protect themselves. It becomes a "way to really talk about the Constitution and your basic rights when you look at what's going on with law enforcement. And," he noted pointedly, "it doesn't cost them anything. We just went to RightOnline in DC," the annual AFP conference. Miller added, "The money we spent was to watch the [Mayweather/Pacquiao] fight."

Had the Romney team cultivated those contacts and built lines of communication into minority communities, he could have perhaps mitigated the damage done by the "47 percent" remark when it emerged in September 2012, and the "safety net" issue from the spring. Miller recalled that Sonnie Johnson, an African American conservative activist and a columnist with Breitbart, tried to work with Romney's campaign to offer a message to deal with the publicity from both remarks, but the campaign didn't listen to her.

As Miller describes Johnson's argument, which she offered repeatedly on her podcasts during the campaign: Romney "could have switched the conversation to 'I'm not talking to the poor, I'm talking to the broke.'" There is a difference, Miller and Johnson argue, between the "broke"—the working poor—and those who live off of entitlements, and their community knows the difference. Republicans have an opening to engage the working poor—"those people that work forty hours a week, pay all their bills, and then don't have nothing else to show for it at the end of the week. That's who I'm talking to."

Another level of frustration comes from seeing statewide Republicans learn the lesson while the national party misses it. In 2008, Pat McCrory narrowly lost the gubernatorial election to Bev Perdue, garnering only 3% of the black vote. McCrory even lost Charlotte, where he had been mayor for fourteen years, winning seven two-year-term elections. Four years later, McCrory had learned his lesson. Among other outreach efforts, his campaign began "sending people into the big Democrat and black churches" to engage in debates with proxies for then–lieutenant governor Walter Dalton, who had won the Democratic primary after Perdue declined to run for another term. McCrory's supporters from the communities in which these events took place undermined arguments from their opponents by noting that they were using the talking points off the campaign website by having attendees check their smartphones during the debate.

With the aggressive engagement, McCrory expanded his

vote among African Americans to 14%, and in 2016 they're aiming for 20%. In North Carolina, and in the nation as a whole, the difference between single digits and double digits in this nearly monolithic bloc of Democratic voters would change election outcomes. Republicans don't assume they'll win the demographic, but they can make inroads that will pay dividends in later cycles by making the effort now. This also gives these communities an investment in both parties that will force them to stop taking for granted that they will vote monolithically in every election. "A big part of it was showing up," one activist noted, "and we didn't traditionally show up."

So far, the national GOP has maintained that tradition to its own detriment, and this stance could be the mistake that causes them to lose Wake County in 2016.

GOING RED IN SMARTSVILLE, USA

North Carolina—and its fifteen electoral votes—have teetered precariously on the red-blue edge for the past two cycles. Republicans cannot afford to give away those votes in 2016. A win in Virginia would not make up for it, nor would carrying Wisconsin or Colorado plus New Hampshire. Besides, a loss of North Carolina would speak to an erosion of Republican and conservative standing in a culture that should provide them with fertile electoral ground.

Republicans and conservatives both like to see themselves as the party that represents small-town America. In the past, both parties have had a claim to that position; but over the last several decades, the Democratic Party has in many ways evolved into a largely urban, coastal party whose biggest support comes from high-density population centers. The GOP has become the party of the rural and exurban areas, competing for the suburbs rather than the cities.

It is difficult to find a swing county that fits the latter description more than Wake. Even the urban center of the county in Raleigh looks more like a small town, with a couple of incongruous steel-and-glass skyscrapers rather than a sprawling collection of them. Cary could serve as a movie location for a period film set in the 1940s or earlier. Culturally, this should be the sweet spot for Republicans.

That environment gives Republicans and conservatives an edge in a county that is growing at record rates. But to take advantage of that culture, Republicans need to find ways to adapt to and attract the younger voters who emerge from the colleges or move here for the high-tech jobs in the Triangle. They can try to win converts from the pilgrims who come looking for a better standard of living, or who come for the education and stay to apply it. But they can also win converts from those who have been in Wake all along—especially those in the African American community—simply by engaging them honestly and openly.

Finally, conservatives can work to get those who have walked away from the GOP to return, people like Don Frantz, who just want to hear inclusiveness from Republicans and their candidates. The Republican nominee can pull together all these disparate strands of voters by focusing on what they have in common—a desire for engagement and economic opportunities—and offering that in positive, optimistic messaging that can restore a sense of hope among Wake County's Republicans.

Wake County gives Republicans and conservatives a real chance to make inroads in a booming high-tech area that still matches their middle-America mind-set, in part by stressing those values of community and outreach. The Republican nominee has to find a way to bridge tradition and the future in a way that appeals to a broad spectrum of voters. But first, as the activist notes, Republicans have to show up, because Democrats already *have*. If Democrats succeed in transforming North Carolina as a beachhead, they will expand that effort to challenge Republican domination throughout the South—and that could cripple Republican and conservative hopes for presidential elections for a very long time to come.

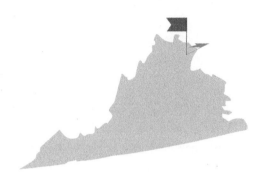

VIRGINIA

PRINCE WILLIAM COUNTY

REPUBLICAN RETREAT OR DEMOCRATIC SURGE?

Virginia's status as a swing state is a relatively recent development. Like most southern states before World War II, it had voted almost entirely Democratic since the end of Reconstruction—but unlike the other southern states, Virginia's vote in national elections shifted to the GOP almost immediately after the war.* Between 1952 and 2004, Democrats won only one presidential election in Virginia: Lyndon Johnson's landslide victory over Barry Goldwater in 1964. Even when southern governors ran for the presidency in 1976, 1992, and 1996, the commonwealth remained firmly Republican.[1]

In the 2004 election,[2] George W. Bush handily won Virginia and its thirteen Electoral College votes as expected, by a 54/46 margin and over 262,000 votes. Four years later, however, Republicans lost the state for the first time in fifty years, with Barack Obama prevailing over John McCain, 53/47, and by 234,000 votes.[3] This was not so much a Republican retreat as it was a Democratic surge. McCain actually got 10,000

---

* The lone exception took place in 1928, when Virginia voted to elect Republican Herbert Hoover.

more votes in Virginia than Bush had in 2004—but Obama added *over a half million votes* to John Kerry's losing effort.

Republicans tried to make a second march on Virginia in 2012 and managed to narrow the gaps—but still lost the state.[4] Mitt Romney gained 97,000 votes over McCain's totals from 2008, but Obama picked up another 12,000 as well, finishing 149,000 votes ahead to win 51/47.

In the aftermath of another defeat for Republicans in Virginia, the *New York Times*'s analysis[5] focused on Republican losses among key emerging demographics in the northern part of the state—particularly in Prince William County, which is located southwest of Washington, DC, and includes the city of Manassas. In 2004, Bush won Prince William by a count of 52.8/46.4, but in 2008, Republican candidates found themselves on the losing end of 57/42 and 57/41 splits—a dramatic reversal from their preceding half century of dominance in the area.

"The Republicans' Southern strategy, of appealing mostly to white voters, appears to have run into a demographic wall," wrote the *Times*'s Michael D. Shear. "If Prince William looks like the future of the country, Democrats have so far developed a much more successful strategy of appealing to that future . . . not only by winning Hispanic voters, but also by winning strong majorities of the growing number of Asian-American voters and of voters under age 40."

Republican Ken Cuccinelli, who ran for governor in 2013 and lost to Democrat Terry McAuliffe, doesn't quite buy that explanation. "I grew up here, I've lived here my whole life," he says, "and we have always—*always*—had a very diverse community here. What's changed the voting pattern isn't people of different ethnicities showing up—it's people moving in who are for big government. If you're one of the 175,000 people [in Northern Virginia] who were sitting at home during the government shutdown two years ago," Cuccinelli argues, "that affects your voting."

In fact, that shutdown took place just weeks ahead of the state elections, which Cuccinelli lost by two and a half points. It's worth noting, though, that the RealClearPolitics polling aggregation in this race[6] shows that Cuccinelli outperformed almost all of the polling in the Virginia gubernatorial race. Even before the shutdown occurred in October, only two of the previous ten polls had McAuliffe leading by less than five points. While it could be true that the shutdown stymied any potential for last-minute momentum, it does not appear to have dramatically changed the race.

Shear also quotes Al Cardenas, chair of the American Conservative Union, warning that conservatives and Republicans need to wake up to the risk of a rout. "Before, we thought it was an important issue, improving demographically," Cardenas told Shear. "Now we know it's an essential issue."

This echoes a similar warning from the Republican National Committee's "autopsy" of the 2012 election. "The pervasive mentality of writing off blocks of states or demographic votes for the Republican Party must be completely forgotten," the report advised. "America is changing demographically, and unless Republicans are able to grow our appeal the way GOP governors have done, the changes tilt the playing field even more in the Democratic direction."

So, what exactly happened in Prince William County, and

in Northern Virginia? And is it possible for Republicans to avoid the demographic fate described by Shear?

NOVA VS. ROVA

Even for the most casual of travelers, history surrounds you the moment you enter Prince William County. Settlers first came to this territory in the early seventeenth century, when a 1608 exploration of the Potomac River demonstrated that the area could support European settlement. By the midcentury, that settlement had pushed out the native Doeg tribes, but it took another eighty-one years for the General Assembly of the Virginia Colony to take portions of Stafford and King George Counties and create Prince William,[7] named after the third son of King George II.

The county's role in the Revolutionary War consisted mainly of maintaining lines of communication for the campaign of 1781. The Marquis de Lafayette brought troops and artillery through Prince William on the King's Highway to reinforce George Washington's army for the decisive Battle of Yorktown.[8] The county had a much more central role in the Civil War, with Manassas playing host to two major battles. It was on the fields of Prince William County that Americans first witnessed the industrialized slaughter that would come to characterize the war.

Today, the battlefield of First Manassas is preserved as a national park. The much larger battlefield of Second Manassas, however, shows little hint of its historical importance and instead has been built up with modern houses, retail malls, hotels, and commercial property. When told where this author was staying, Virginia House of Delegates member Jackson Miller remarked, "You're literally on the land where lines were forming and fighting each other" in Second Manassas.

The history of the Civil War battlefields in Manassas and elsewhere in Prince William gives a certain flavor to the area, says former Virginia attorney general Ken Cuccinelli, but doesn't comprise its entire identity. "That heritage, that history is still part of the personality of the county," Cuccinelli says, but "it's not a focal point, it's not a flash point. There is a sense that this is an old county," he continues, "but that's a positive here."

Thanks to roaring growth in Prince William County since the end of World War II, history no longer mixes with the present; it has faded from view, if not from memory. For Republicans, that sums up their loss of Virginia as a GOP stronghold—it has not faded from memory, but for more than a decade, it has been difficult to imagine that those days might return.

Prince William County has had strong economic and population growth for most of the last 150 years.[9] The last time a decennial census showed a decrease in population was 1870, when the Civil War resulted in a net loss for 12.4% of the county's residents, falling back to 7,504. Even with steady and sometimes double-digit growth in every decade in between, Prince William County's population on the eve of World War II remained at only 17,738.

The rapid expansion of the military in the 1940s and the Cold War's demand for a strong defense produced a boom in the county that has yet to end. The population doubled in the 1950s—and then doubled again in the '60s as the federal government continued to expand. By 1970, more than 111,000 people lived in Prince William County. By 2010, the population had nearly quadrupled to 402,000—and, four years after that, the Census Bureau showed an increase of 46,000 people. Just the increase in those four years is more than double the county's entire population in 1950.

Needless to say, this growth was hardly organic. As the federal government expanded, its workers flocked to Northern Virginia, where they could live within commuting range of the District of Columbia. Those workers, whether employed by a government agency or federal contractors, came from every corner of the United States to settle in Arlington, Fairfax, Prince William, and Loudoun Counties, and this created a cultural and political split within the state. Northern Virginia—or NOVA, as Virginians call it—has a distinct personality and culture from the rest of Virginia, or ROVA.

One important difference between NOVA and ROVA is the eye-popping rankings of median household income levels in the former. A 2011 Census Bureau study put Prince William County seventh in the nation for median household income, at $95,146,[10] and by 2014 it had risen to $98,071. The median household income level for Virginia as a whole comes to $63,907—well above the national average of $53,046, but much farther away from that of Prince William County.

The more shocking revelation was that this didn't even earn Prince William County a *bronze* medal in the 2011 NOVA income Olympics. The top three counties in the nation for household income were, in order: Loudoun ($119,134), Fairfax ($105,797), and Arlington ($100,735). Just behind Prince

William came two other adjacent NOVA counties, Fauquier (eighth) and Stafford (thirteenth). The report set off a firestorm of controversy over the size of government and the fact that the area surrounding Washington, DC, was enjoying an economic boom during the height of the Great Recession.

By other demographic measures, too, Prince William County differs from the state as a whole. First, PWC tends to be younger than the state and the country. Of its population, 8.3% are seniors, almost half the rate of the United States (14.5%) and five points below Virginia's rate. Children make up somewhat more of the population in Prince William County—28.1% to 22.4% for Virginia—so the overall effect is to have nearly the same percentage of working-age adults, 63.6% to 63.8% for the state. The net impact, though, is a community more inclined to focus on the future, and a county that will continue to expand its voting presence for many cycles to come.

The ethnic mix in Prince William County makes it unique, too. The expansion of the last four years has brought more white residents, with their percentage of the population rising from 57.8% to 64.4%, still well below the state and national averages of 70.5% and 77.4%. African Americans make up 21.5% of the population, ahead of Virginia's 19.7% and the nation's 13.2%. Asians, another growing population, make up 8.4% of Prince William County residents, two points ahead of the state's rate and three points ahead of the national population.

The Hispanic population makes up a surprising 22% of the population, almost triple the percentage of Virginia as a whole. That is a larger percentage of the population than in

Jefferson County, Colorado, another heavily Hispanic battle-ground county discussed later in the book. Many of these Hispanics work in the construction trade, attracted by the rapid growth of Prince William County, whose economy includes very little in the way of agriculture.

"It's an extremely diverse community," says Jackson Miller, "more so than [Democratic Party stronghold] Fairfax, which is the irony. We're one of the fastest-growing counties," Miller continues, "so many Latino families move here for the construction industry—and as this area boomed, they all came to do the work."

Immigrants come to do the work in part because they're motivated by the opportunity for success, and in part because the area's longtime residents aren't willing to do hard physical work, says Tito Muñoz. A Colombian immigrant in the late 1970s, Muñoz rose to national fame in the 2008 election as "Tito the Builder," an unashamed conservative entrepreneur who joined Sarah Palin on the campaign trail. In these appearances, Muñoz leveraged his personal story of going from having nothing and holding down several jobs at a time to owning companies of his own.

"We don't have young people there," Muñoz says about his employees. "I had a teenager kid working for me for the summer but I don't have no twenty-twos, no twenty-fives working in the construction. They don't want to work for fifteen dollars over there, you know, sweating at ninety degrees and shoveling." Muñoz shrugs. "Now immigrants, on the other hand, they have no choice" but to work hard to get ahead, especially if they don't speak English well enough to find other work. Muñoz proudly points out that he took that same path to reach his American dream, and he wants to help others achieve it as well.

The need for construction labor reflects the opportunities created by Prince William County's rapid expansion. However, the bulk of the community's employment still comes from the county government and Washington, DC. The county's annual financial report for fiscal year 2013/14[11] lists the major employers of its residents, and two of its top five are the Department of Defense and the Morale, Welfare and Recreation network, which is operated on behalf of active-duty military, veterans, and their families. The county report specifies only that all of its top six employers have "more than 1,000" employees in Prince William, but the two military employers are ranked second and fifth, respectively. The only private employer in the county's top five is Walmart. (Prince William County School Board is the county's top employer.)

The report notes that the county struggles with being a bedroom community for Washington, DC: "Despite progress in attracting jobs to the County, Prince William continues to export nearly two-thirds (63.8%) of its labor force to jobs outside the county, accounting for the fifteenth longest commute in the United States." Cuccinelli, who grew up in Prince William County, confirms that this has been a major issue in its rapid growth.

"Prince William is really two different counties," he says. "You've got the northern and western part, which is really a high-growth suburbia. Then you've got the southern and eastern part, which is the Route 1 Corridor—heavily minority populated, votes much more heavily in federal elections," compared with turnout in the odd-year state elections.

State delegate Scott Lingamfelter splits Prince William along Interstate 95. "The I-95 Corridor, which is the eastern end of the county, tends to be more Democratic," he says. "When you begin to move to the west, it becomes decisively Republican." Former RNC chair and senatorial candidate Ed Gillespie calls the cultural divide along I-95 a key part of understanding Prince William County, and to winning the state. "The fulcrum of the commonwealth is probably right there."

WILD IRISH NOVA

Few observers expected Democrats to have a good showing in the 2014 midterms, but few also expected the Republicans to succeed as much as they did. Republicans gained eight Senate seats and picked up a handful of House seats from Democrats, taking full control of Congress for the first time since 2006.

But in Virginia, the biggest surprise of all came in a race that a Republican ended up losing. Mark Warner (D), the popular former governor, appeared to be poised for a second term in the Senate despite the woes of Democrats elsewhere in the country. Republicans had nominated former RNC chair Ed Gillespie, who had served in George W. Bush's administration and had founded a lobbying firm and a political consultancy. In a Tea Party era, Gillespie looked like everything grassroots conservatives either opposed, or at least wouldn't support with any particular *enthusiasm*.

Polling for the race showed a blowout on the horizon.

The RealClearPolitics average[12] showed Warner up almost ten points on the eve of the election, but even that large gap underestimated Warner's dominance. Polls had narrowed in October—although only one poll that month showed Gillespie within single-digit range of Warner—but throughout the summer, Gillespie had trailed by as much as twenty-five points in the well-regarded Roanoke College poll. The disparity spooked donors and organizations outside of Virginia and pushed them to invest in more competitive races.

On Election Day, Gillespie proved that to be perhaps a fatal error. Gillespie spent most of the night leading as precincts reported their vote totals, only having his lead slip away when the Democratic stronghold of Fairfax added its full vote totals to the mix. Instead of a ten-point-or-more blowout, Warner won Virginia with only a narrow plurality, 49/48.[13] Gillespie also closed the gap in Prince William, but just barely missed the mark, losing 48/50 by a 2,722-vote advantage. All told, Gillespie came in fewer than 17,000 votes shy of what would have been by far the night's biggest upset.

How did Gillespie almost steal Virginia's Senate seat from Warner? The key was outreach in communities outside the Republican Party's normal comfort zone, Gillespie says, emphasizing his own experience as a first-generation American. "I am the son of an immigrant myself, and would make that point in these communities," Gillespie recalls. "My father came here as a boy from Ireland. My grandfather was a janitor, and I got to grow up to be counselor to the president of the United States of America." He used that experience as an entrée to these communities, emphasizing his desire to duplicate it for their families. "I want the same opportunities for future generations," he told them during his campaign.

Gillespie also focused on themes and issues that resonated across community lines, emphasizing "upward mobility and job creation, economic growth, lifting people out of poverty, and higher wages," as well as "education, a reform-and-replace plan for ObamaCare, energy production, and more affordable energy." More important than the message itself was where and how Gillespie communicated it.

"I went into the black churches in Prince William, and to places a lot of Republicans have not gone," he says. County Republican Party vice chair D. J. Jordan, a leading African American conservative in Prince William, corroborates this. "Grace Church Dumfries is a church that Ed Gillespie visited in October 2014," Jordan recalls, "and he was very well received. They welcomed him from the pulpit and he was able to talk to those who were out in the lobby afterwards."

Gillespie also targeted communities that speak languages other than English, preparing campaign materials in seven different languages. Gillespie notes that this made an impact even with people who spoke and read English well: "I had my campaign literature translated into Spanish language as well as Korean and Tagalog and Vietnamese." Gillespie recalls the positive reaction at one Korean festival. "A lot of the people I was handing it to were bilingual and could easily have taken the English version of my campaign material. But they liked the fact that I had gone to the trouble to translate it into the Korean language. It's the manifestation of a welcoming campaign."

Did it have an impact? Exit polling from the 2012 and 2014 elections[14] certainly suggests that it did. Gillespie showed some marginal improvement in the African American vote over Romney, moving from 93/6 to 90/9, even while the ethnic turnout model remained almost identical. The 2014 midterms had a sharp drop-off in turnout for younger voters—from 19% of the electorate in 2012 to 12%—but Warner only beat Gillespie 50/39; two years earlier, Obama won that demographic 61/36. More ominously for Democrats, 11% of younger voters declined to cast a ballot for any Senate candidate, while only 3% had declined to cast a ballot in the presidential race two years earlier.

Gillespie's strong showing prompted an avalanche of what-ifs within the GOP, and it provides a road map for the presidential nominee in 2016. Following that map will take a concerted and sustained effort by the presidential campaign to reach the communities on both sides of the I-95 divide. "I was very well received, warmly received," Gillespie says. "But the truth is you are more warmly received the second time you show up—and even more warmly received the third time."

BUILDING FRANCHISES

Tito Muñoz and his wife, Deborah, took a rare weekend afternoon off to discuss the problems with Republican outreach in Prince William County. "I've been working seven days a week, with Saturdays and Sundays, and I still have to work at home," Tito says as we sit in the Todos Supermarket in Wood-bridge, near the southeastern end of Prince William. "Look, in America that's what it takes. If I want to grow my company, that's what it takes to do it."

Todos itself could be called a manifestation of the American dream that Muñoz describes. A large modern supermarket filled with gleaming aisles and plenty of customers, it also features a ready-to-eat food counter in the back, with booths and tables for eating and sitting. Todos is more than just a supermarket, though; it's a one-stop center for the needs of the heavily Hispanic neighborhood that surrounds it.[15] It offers financial services such as check cashing and bill payments, a Nationwide insurance office, a travel agency, notary and tax preparation services, and more.

Tito explains that Carlos Castro, owner of the supermarket, came to the United States as a refugee from El Salvador's civil war and initially went to work in construction. But he soon began looking for another way to reach his version of the American dream. "He said, 'Man, Tito, I cannot work in construction. I'm a little thin, the shovel is too heavy for me,'" Tito recalls. "So he started selling groceries in a truck." Today, Castro owns two supermarkets, with hundreds of employees and English classes offered on-site.

During the 2012 campaign, Republicans invited Castro to meet with them. Castro was appreciative of the effort but wondered why they didn't come to the supermarket and the neighborhood it services. "He said, okay, this is all well and good," Deborah recalls, "but why won't they just come into my store and talk to my employees?"

As it happens, Todos Supermarket *was* a stop for Gillespie during his Senate bid. "I was there," Gillespie says, and "it was fun."

Tito and Deborah have long served as ambassadors for the conservative and Republican message. While out campaigning in the neighborhoods, Tito would start discussing the issues at people's doors, but "they said no, come inside the house and sit in the living room." After about perhaps fifteen to twenty minutes, residents would often invite more people over. "Now the daughter comes, and then the husband. I mean, now I have like six people there, six voters."

"That's time consuming," Tito admits, "but it has to be done. If you're able to do that, you can reach twenty to thirty families, then later you create an event. And then they invite friends."

Sometimes, though, the Muñozes feel betrayed by the tone Republicans use on immigration and other issues. "Dick Armey [former House Majority Leader and conservative activist] has a fantastic quote," Deborah says. " 'You don't tell a girl she's ugly, and then ask her to the prom.' " The problem between conservatives and the Hispanic community became especially acute in 2007,[16] when Prince William County passed an ordinance that allowed police to check on legal resident status when detained—a move that humiliated legal residents. It was later repealed, Deborah notes, but the damage was done.

"I'm not a Mexican," says Tito, "but my workers are Mexicans, and I have friends who are Mexicans. I don't want them to insult my friends. I don't want them to insult the children of my friends, you know what I mean?"

Sonnie Johnson, a Breitbart News contributor and conservative African American activist in Prince William County, puts it more strongly when discussing the GOP's approach. "It is not safe for me to put a reputation that I am trying to build in my community into your hands. It is not safe. And I won't do it," she says.

For one thing, Johnson feels pressure to abandon her culture in order to fit into the GOP. "Yes, it's a big tent, but that don't mean all of the blacks want to listen to country music." Like most millennials, she listens to a wide variety of genres, including hip-hop and rap, a music and culture that generates disapproval and scorn among Republicans. "If you wanted liberty or freedom, you wouldn't care what kind of music I listen to, as long as I wasn't taking nothing from the system. I've contributed *back* to the system. I'm not taking anything from it. Why does it matter to you what I listen to?"

The core issue, though, for Johnson, is the way in which Republicans think they can simply renew a relationship that they abandoned decades ago. "I'm not talking about slavery. I'm not talking about whips and chains," she says. "I'm talking about you letting progressives take over the education system. I'm talking about you letting unions build power and taking away from public spending locally. I'm talking about you letting them pass all of these fees, fines, rules, regulations that strip any feeling of freedom away whatsoever." The consequences of this betrayal, Johnson says, are felt in the black community every day.

Johnson analogizes the GOP's approach toward black voters to a father who walks out on his family. "Now you want to come back when the child is grown and say, 'Let me tell you how to run your life,' and you didn't even come back say-ing, 'I'm sorry I left.' And you don't understand why there's a problem?"

The GOP wants a do-over, Johnson says, but this means they must start by admitting that they were wrong. "Once you saw that you could have power without us, as long as that power could be obtained, you didn't care. Now admit it. Admit it! And say it to black people, we did this," Johnson says. "My party did this. We ignored. We walked away from our history. We walked away from what we built. We turned our backs on the principles that we value in our guts . . . and that was our fault."

Until Republicans come back to the African American community with sincere repentance for that abandonment, Johnson says, "none of that other stuff matters."

D. J. Jordan, vice chair of the county's Republican party, is more optimistic about the prospects of outreach. A onetime producer for CNN and Fox in Washington, DC, and a ris-ing star in GOP circles, the African American conservative sees Prince William as an opportunity for Republicans to win back a diverse community—if they make the effort to reach for it.

"My neighborhood is probably a really good representa-tion of Prince William County," Jordan says. "We have folks from India, we have African Americans, we have Caucasians, we have Asians on my street. There's a lot of children, and we all get along very well, and everyone plays together very well: it's beautiful to see. Everyone lives together in that type of harmony."

Like the Muñozes, Jordan finds that the first issue he

hears when it comes to engaging with overlooked communities isn't policy—it's *tone*. "When I'm engaging minority communities," he says, "they say, 'You know, some of what Republicans stand for, I actually agree with. But I just can't vote for them, because I feel like they don't want me to be part of the party. I feel like you guys are so angry and you are not inclusive, I just feel like you don't want anything to do with me in that community.' We hear that a lot," Jordan laments.

Trying to move past tone by talking strictly about policy or ideology doesn't work, Jordan says, because it ignores how people make their voting decisions. "Most American voters vote based on likability and association," he explains, "and that's most Americans *period*, not just minority voters." Republicans who want to start building support in these communities have to understand that trust comes first.

Solving the tone problem would allow the house-by-house strategy to work in favor of Republicans, Tito Muñoz argues, in a kind of franchise operation. Rather than bringing in people to put out the same message to everyone, Republicans should ask themselves, "How can we explain our agenda in a way that addresses the concerns of that community, and then how can we find Tito and Debbie to go out and help us to make that case?" he says. "We have a plan for uplifting people out of poverty. That's our message." All we need are the franchisees.

WALKING THE LINE

Walking a neighborhood with state delegate Rich Anderson takes more energy than one might first imagine. Anderson, sixty, has more spring in his step than a man twenty years younger, in part because he enjoys any chance to meet his constituents where they live. On this day, Anderson is walking a neighborhood for his wife, Ruth, who is running for a local office. "When she's not with me," Anderson jokes with constituents, "I'm Ruth-less."

Door knocking has advanced by leaps and bounds over the last few decades. Rather than clipboards and notepads, candidates now use smartphones to link up with large databases through apps like i360. These combine commercially available data and GPS pinpoint locations with information gleaned through door knocking in order to build voter profiles that will be critical in the get-out-the-vote process in the days before an election. Anderson dutifully logs the information from each house, even noting if no one answered and what material was left at the door.

It's about more than just data for Anderson. He genuinely enjoys meeting and getting to know his constituents, even when things go amiss. In his first campaign, a voter invited Anderson into the house to continue the conversation but left him alone for a few moments with her small dog—who promptly bit down on Anderson's pants cuff. Anderson managed to free himself before the voter came back to the room and hid the torn cuff during the conversation. He had the pants repaired and now wears that suit on the first day of each legislative session. "It reminds me to stay humble," he explains.

Anderson offers pointers as we walk the neighborhood, such as checking bumper stickers and banners to get a sense of each household's political leanings. On today's walk, people's reactions—at least those who are home on this Labor Day weekend, which aren't many—range from nonplussed to enthusiastic. One couple, pulling out of their driveway, waits in the car to greet Rich warmly once they see him walking the sidewalk. None is displeased to see Rich, and a couple offer their thoughts on their issue priorities—mostly the economy, veteran's issues, and national defense.

Presidential candidates can't walk every neighborhood, of course, but their campaigns must talk to people on this granular level in order to connect. "You got to ask for everyone to vote," says Jordan. "You can't look at past polling data and say, 'In order to scoop up 51 percent, fifty plus one, we have to talk to *these* people.' It doesn't work that way anymore." In fact, Jordan says, it hasn't worked that way in Prince William for a long time—at least for the last decade or more. "Ed Gillespie almost pulled off a great upset against a very popular incumbent senator by doing exactly that, by going to talk to everyone," Jordan recalls. "We need to go after every single vote."

To do that, says state delegate Scott Lingamfelter, the campaign needs to partner with people who know Prince William. He's seen what happens otherwise. "You hire some guy out of Milwaukee or some guy out of Tallahassee or some guy out of Little Rock who you know you feel good about," Lingamfelter says, "and they're as clueless as a pig looking at a Timex watch." He thinks the presidential nominee should also do at least a *little* door knocking, a suggestion he made to one primary candidate.

"They said, what do you think we ought to do? And I said, well, send that man to me and I'll go door to door," Lingamfelter recalls. "And they said, are you serious—a presidential candidate? I said, yeah. We'll run around, take some coffee together, knock on the doors. I would say, 'I'm Scott Lingamfelter, I'm running for delegate, and this is [candidate name] and he is running for president, what you got to say to him?' " Lingamfelter laughs. "You could probably hardly get in the car for knocking down the cameras and the media." This would have a huge impact on voters in these communities, Lingamfelter says, for very little effort. "If he knocked on a hundred doors in Prince William County, he could walk away and say, you know what, I've got the pulse of this place."

THE BEST OFFENSE IS A GOOD DEFENSE

At some point, policy *will* matter. Republicans need to speak to the issues that matter most—and avoid the pitfalls of antagonizing voters. That concern over tone doesn't just apply to addressing minority communities in Prince William County; it also has to do with the broad way in which they communicate the traditional conservative and Republican missions of reducing the size of federal government.

In most other states, this idea sells like hotcakes. But Prince William County's economy relies in large part, directly or indirectly, on the federal government, so the kind of message on government waste that would do well in states like Texas, Utah, and Alaska could spell box-office poison for Republicans in NOVA. The area is too economically sensitive to budget reductions to enthusiastically embrace a slash-and-cut message—and its large number of veterans will focus on national defense as a priority.

For retired army officer Doug Morrison, the most pressing issue is defense-budget sequestration, and he believes many of Prince William's veterans see it as a high priority as well. "It is not how one governs; it's not how you have a coherent strategy," Morrison says. Since the passage of the Bipartisan Budget Act of 2013, the US position around the world has been in retreat. "When that legislation was passed in December of 2013, Ukraine hadn't happened," Morrison says. "We had not seen the upheaval and disintegration in the Mideast and North Africa, the rise of ISIS. So fundamentally," he concludes, "you have legislation in place [that] doesn't reflect reality."

State delegate Rich Anderson agrees that defense and national security issues will take a large part in voter decisions, and for the same reasons. "About 50 percent of my district are veterans," he explains, adding that the fight over budgets and especially sequestration will be particularly provocative in Prince William. "Sequestration has hit this area very hard. Northern Virginia is no longer the economic generator for the state," Anderson explains, and what Republicans do about it will matter in 2016.

On the other hand, much of the need for sequestration came from out-of-control federal expansion that Republicans oppose. Cuccinelli points out the conundrum for Republicans looking to recapture the county. "Let's be really blunt," he says. "What drives the growth around here—on a bipartisan basis—is big government. And big-government people tend to vote for big government."

One former statewide-office candidate believes that the same message can sell with a different argument—and tone, for that matter. "Using the term 'federal bureaucrats' is like nails on the chalkboard to them," he says. "A lot of these workers are FBI agents, DEA agents, or even air traffic controllers who work at the Pentagon. They will vote for Republicans if you don't poke them in the eye with a sharp stick."

The former candidate also thinks that framing it as a free-market policy works better in Prince William County than the approach demonizing government agencies. "Say the federal government is doing too many things that are better left to the private sector or state and local governments, and failing at too many things the federal government ought to get right. A lot of it, again, is tone."

GOING RED IN THE COMMONWEALTH

Using the word "battleground" to describe Prince William County takes on a kind of irony, considering the history of this region. Still, the NOVA region has given Democrats most of their success over the last decade in Virginia, and its continuing growth makes it essential for Republicans to improve their standing there.

"Putting your finger on Prince William County is pretty astute," Ed Gillespie says, noting that he lost it by only a few hundred votes in his surprising 2014 Senate bid. "It is a critically important area for carrying Virginia," he continues, "which is critically important to any Republican when in the White House. It is very diverse, it's diverse geographically and demographically in every way."

It's that diversity that makes Prince William a real bell-wether, not just in Virginia but also for other swing counties with large minority populations. The only way to carry Prince William is to find votes to add to Republican totals and to outpace Democratic efforts to hold on to the coalition that Barack Obama was able to bring together. Obama's retirement gives Republicans an opportunity to reestablish their relationships with these voters, perhaps most notable in African American communities, but with Hispanics as well. Freed from the obligation to run *against* Obama, an inspirational and charismatic figure, Republicans and conservatives can bring voters a more positive agenda.

Gillespie's candidacy shows the possibilities of a ground-focused campaign in Prince William and in Northern Virginia. "I got the second-highest percentage of the black vote for a Republican Senate candidate in the country," he says, "second to Tim Scott, the first black Republican senator in the South since Reconstruction." It was a modest 10%, but still an improvement from Romney's 6% in 2012. "I got 15 percent of African American males, according to the NBC exit surveys. I split the Asian American vote 50/50."

Those are numbers that Republicans need on a national basis in order to compete. If the presidential contender can make it work in Prince William, not only would that portend a victory in Virginia, it would suggest that a number of other states could move from blue to red in 2016.

WISCONSIN

BROWN COUNTY

TITLETOWN, USA

The peaceful farmland of Brown County, Wisconsin, belies its status as a political battleground. For more than thirty years, Democrats and Republicans have fought bitterly here, at every level of government, for offices and for their ideological agendas. Rarely seen as a key state in terms of its vote totals, Wisconsin nevertheless has a habit of making national headlines and attracting the attention of strategists.

The name of Brown County, Wisconsin, might not be terribly familiar, but its urban center of Green Bay will be familiar to anyone who has watched a National Football League game. The city calls itself "Titletown, USA" in honor of the thirteen league championships the team has accumulated since its founding in 1919, including four Super Bowl victories. When the NFL first formed in the 1920s, small-town teams like the Packers were more common, but eventually they moved to cities that had larger venues and bigger populations to support them—or folded up and disappeared. The Packers, named for one of the biggest industries in this city on the coast of Lake Michigan, stayed put and became Green Bay's identity.

However, the Packers almost didn't live long enough to win a title at all. Four years after they formed, the team faced bankruptcy, owing to the volatile environment of professional football's infancy. "Rather than fold," however, wrote Dave Zirin in a profile for the *New Yorker*,[1] "they decided to sell shares to the community, with fans each throwing down a couple of dollars to keep the team afloat. That humble frozen seed has since blossomed into a situation wherein more than a hundred thousand stockholders own more than four million shares of a perennial playoff contender."

To this day, the Green Bay Packers are the only US major-sport franchise to have community ownership, a point of considerable pride for the city. At Lambeau Field, the team's logo—a giant "G"—towers over the modest Green Bay skyline and can be seen for miles on Interstate 41 as one approaches the city from the south. From the north, the stadium's Jumbotron can be seen when the Packers are playing.

Zirin called the Packers a "hardscrabble team," a description that applies to Green Bay, if not to Brown County in general. The population of Green Bay barely breaks into six figures, at just under 105,000,[2] and accounts for 40% of the population of Brown County (256,670). Green Bay's median household income level falls well below the national average of $53,046 at $42,247, even though Brown County's median income level slightly exceeds the national average at $53,119. The poverty level shifts significantly between Green Bay (17.8%) and the county (12.1%), straddling the national average of 14.5%.

Outside of Green Bay, suburban villages such as Bellevue, Howard, Ashwaubenon, and Allouez show recent investment and growth in both business and residential capacity. Since the 1960s, most of Brown County's expansion has taken place in these first-ring suburbs. In the last twenty-five years, Brown's population has grown almost 32%, compared with 8.7% growth in Green Bay during the same period.

Some of that growth comes from the expansion of industry, especially in the tech sector. Mike Bruno, a young Chicago transplant, lives in the upscale town of Bellevue and sees more out-of-state hires moving into Brown County, and into his apartment complex. "They came up here for work," he says, and most of the work in Brown County is found in Green Bay's suburbs.

That creates a difference between traditional Brown County voters and the new transplants. The latter's focus on politics is "more on the macro level, on national politics," according to Bruno. They bring their political leanings from their places of origin, which is why it's no surprise that the biggest turnarounds in Brown County between the 2004 and 2008 elections were in these first-ring suburbs—especially in Howard, De Pere, and Bellevue.

UNNECESSARY ROUGHNESS

Republicans have long felt that they were on the cusp of turning Wisconsin red in a national election. Ever since 1984, when Ronald Reagan won Wisconsin in a forty-nine-state landslide, the GOP has tried to put the Badger State solidly in the red column. In 2004, Republicans thought they had actually pulled it off, but John Kerry managed to eke out an 11,384-vote win[3]—mostly by running up his vote totals in Dane and Milwaukee Counties, the most populous urban centers in Wisconsin.

By 2008, any dreams of winning Wisconsin had been crushed. Wisconsin delivered a blowout win for Barack Obama in his first presidential bid, taking the state by thirteen points and almost 415,000 votes.[4] Obama's dominance even extended to the northeastern quadrant of Wisconsin, which normally trends center right. Republican ambitions for the state appeared to be on life support, if not entirely dead.

Two years later, though, a combination of state and national discontent resuscitated those hopes. Scott Walker, a conservative Milwaukee County executive, led Republicans to an impressive sweep, capturing the legislature and the gubernatorial race in a surprisingly easy 52/46 win. The Republican sweep surprised many and put Wisconsin back on the map of hotly contested presidential battlegrounds.

First, other battles would be fought in Wisconsin, with increasing vitriol and bitterness. Walker immediately seized the momentum to push for the law that became known as Act 10, a reform of public-employee union (PEU) bargaining laws that stripped PEUs (other than for first responders) of bargaining rights for benefit packages. Wisconsin, which had a strong history of support for unions, prepared for battle, but few could have guessed at the scope or the depth of the division to come.

When it became apparent that Republicans had the votes to pass Act 10, thousands of union activists flocked to Madison in an attempt to shut down the legislature. Democratic legislators bolted the state in an attempt to deny Republicans a quorum, holing up in motels across the border in Illinois to evade arrest and transport back to the capital. For weeks, demonstrators refused to leave, and elected Democrats refused to return, and the story ran at the top of the national news every day.

Walker refused to back down or to negotiate with Democrats as long as they remained out of state. Finally, the Democratic delegation returned and Act 10 passed almost immediately. Walker signed it into law, and after a court challenge from the PEUs failed, it went into effect.* The unions fought back, pushing Democrats into a rare gubernatorial recall election in an attempt to win a chance to repeal Act 10. Both sides raised tens of millions of dollars, and Tom Barrett won a primary to get a second shot at Walker in June 2012, five months before the presidential election. No governor had ever withstood a recall . . . until Walker. He cruised to a 53/47 win[5] over Barrett, a similar margin to the election of 2010.†

The wide margin of Walker's victory, combined with the massive outlay of union cash in a futile recall bid, raised hopes even further that Republicans could finally win Wis-

---

* Not only did Walker turn out to be correct about the budget savings, it turned out that many PEU members chose not to pay dues. Four years later, the Wisconsin Education Association's membership had dropped by a third, while the American Federation of Teachers membership rolls had been cut in half. The number of union members among Wisconsin state employees dropped by 70 percent.

† Two years later, Walker would beat Mary Burke in the regular gubernatorial cycle to win a second term, again with a similar margin of victory at 52/47.

consin's electoral votes in 2012. Walker had put together a massive get-out-the-vote effort, an organization that many assumed could be passed as a turnkey operation to Mitt Romney and the GOP. And in a tight race, Wisconsin's votes might make the difference, especially since Romney's team remained confident that they could take back several key states from Obama, including Florida, Ohio, Indiana, and North Carolina.

Unfortunately for Romney and the Republican Party, the momentum built in Walker's recall victory appeared to evaporate in less than five months. Obama got 57,000 fewer votes than in 2008, and Romney added 158,000 Republican votes to McCain's total. But Obama still cruised to a 53/46 win—ironically, the same margin by which Walker beat the recall.[6]

How did Republicans manage to lose Wisconsin when, by all appearances, they were the ones with momentum? How did Barack Obama take Wisconsin despite its rousing endorsement of Walker five months earlier?

Congressman Reid Ribble argues that the result came from the unique circumstances of the recall, and the electorate that showed up for it. His 8th Congressional District covers all of Brown County, and he heard from Democrats and independents who thought the recall was unfair. "They believed that the recall should have been if Governor Walker had done something that had been illegal or there had been some malfeasance," Ribble says, "but on principle they just said you don't remove the governor or overturn an election because you don't have his policy. So there were a lot of Democrats and independents that supported Governor Walker in that recall on that basis alone."

Conservative talk radio show host Jerry Bader, a well-known voice in Green Bay, concurs—at least in part. Governor Walker's showing in the recall was "driven in part by people who maybe disagreed with Act 10 but who really disagreed with the notion of taking him out of office over an issue dispute," Bader says.

There are other key differences, too. The recall was a match between bitter rivals in a minor league, while the presidential election pitted a championship team in a league of its own against an overmatched upstart.

GOING DEEP

To understand how to compete in Brown County, it's important to know *why* Brown County holds such strategic importance for Republicans. The state's two main urban centers, Milwaukee and the state capital of Madison, tilt heavily Democratic. Even in Scott Walker's three relatively easy election victories, he lost Milwaukee County and Dane County (Madison) by enormous margins. (In his 2014 reelection, for example, Mary Burke won 63% of the Milwaukee County vote, and 70% in Dane.)

In order to counter the heavy Democratic advantage in the state's most populous counties, Republicans need to win a large number of votes from smaller counties, especially in the northern and eastern quadrants of Wisconsin. The map of their current slate of House Representatives from the 2014 election, when Republicans won five of Wisconsin's eight seats, gives a good indication of how the GOP needs to perform in order to win the Badger State's ten Electoral College votes.

Brown County sits almost in the middle of the eastern half of Wisconsin. Its position, plus the importance of the Green Bay television market—which covers much of the eastern part of Wisconsin—makes Brown a bellwether for the statewide race. "Brown County is often seen as the swing county in the swing part of the state," political analyst Kevin Binversie says.

While Milwaukee and Dane carry much more of a partisan and ideological tilt, Brown's voters tend to be more independent. "It's very rural, so it's very community focused in the sense that it's neighbors helping neighbors," Binversie explains, and warns that government cuts for the sake of cutting alone won't sell well in Brown. "We want government that's frugal, but also gets the job done."

Ribble, who has won Brown County by substantial margins in all three of his elections, agrees that the ideological approach won't work there. "What citizens of Brown County want is pragmatism. I've heard repeatedly, *just solve the problem.*" Ribble points out that almost a third of Brown County voters are independents who "just absolutely abhor the vindictive style of political campaigning."

Previous so-called base strategies won't cut it in Brown County, according to Ribble. Romney won Brown County in 2012, but Obama's "more positive tone" in advertising limited the Republican nominee's ability to build a big lead, and to extend it throughout the eastern half of the state. "That's why Romney didn't move further ahead than he did," Ribble says. "To win Wisconsin, you've got to win Brown County by twelve points."

To do that, though, the presidential campaign will have to engage with voters, and those who know them. Ribble won Brown by twelve points in 2012, but the Romney campaign "certainly weren't engaged with me," Ribble says. With fellow Republican congressman Paul Ryan on the ticket, Ribble assumes that the Romney campaign felt they had enough insight to win the state without making local connections, but the end result was a missed opportunity, especially on messaging.

"It was all national messaging," Ribble recalls. Brown County voters want to know the candidate as a person, but the Romney campaign didn't satisfy that desire. "They certainly didn't capture the personality, the compassion, the thoughtfulness that Governor Romney showed. They didn't capture his personal integrity, his forty-year marriage, the family that is philanthropic," Ribble says. "Those are the types of things that would have resonated with this fairly staunchly religious area."

It takes more than just messaging, says Mark Graul, a political consultant who has worked state and national elections in Wisconsin since the early 1990s. The difference, especially in 2012, was the extraordinary ability of Barack Obama's campaign to turn out voters, not just message to them.

"The numbers that Barack Obama did in rural Wisconsin in 2008 were unbelievable," Graul says. "There was a lot of belief that the Democrats were the party for the middle class and for working families, whereas Republicans were just for the big-business guys and the bailouts and things of that nature."

By 2012, this optimism had faded, which made Obama's near win in Brown all the more surprising. "The reason why Obama got 49 percent of the vote in Brown County was purely an organizational muscle that they flexed," Graul says. "We didn't realize how good they were at turning out non-traditional voters." He underscores this point by contrasting the November 2012 results with the recall results five months prior. "Walker got 61,969 in June, and Romney got 64,000. So you see that Romney got a few more votes than Walker did, just from the presidential year turnout. But Barrett got 41,000, and Obama got 62,000. So, not even 3,000, 2,000 more Republican votes from June to November—and 20,000 more Democrat votes. That's turnout. That's flat-out Obama machine turnout that was not there for the recall."

In other words, Romney really never stood a chance of winning Wisconsin or any of the other swing states that Obama's campaign prioritized. The Obama campaign had built their organization from the neighborhood level up and knew how to reach voters who only occasionally turn out for elections. Marian Krumberger, a retired social worker who has become a conservative political activist, recalls witnessing the groundwork that produced this extraordinary turnout. "[Democrats] come in with their white iPads and go in the neighborhoods," she says. "They know there's certain houses they have, and they target the people who only vote every four years. And they vote Democrat."

In the recall, the GOP worked hard on GOTV, and Krumberger participated in the effort. "A lot of our Republicans, our Brown County folks here, never received phone calls from the party before," she says. "That phone call was very effective during the recall. We called them. I think I made 30,000 calls myself." At the end of it, though, Krumberger got the same sense of fatigue that Jessika Olson saw among the activists. "Once we moved on, people who worked on the campaign got sick of these phone calls."

Krumberger warns that the state Democratic Party will be ready to repeat their performance in 2016. "They're backed by the national [party], and they come in, and so it's a little bit scary. We're going to have to really get out. We've got big competition here."

But will Democrats be able to reconstitute that effort? For some insight into that question, we need to ask someone closer to the source.

SCOUTING THE OPPOSITION

"Bill" has immersed himself in Democratic politics from childhood, describing himself as "a junkie" who "grew up in the business . . . literally." During his childhood, his parents were activists in the Democratic Party, and they often had high-ranking Democratic officeholders come to the house, sometimes putting them up for the night. As a boy, Bill took that somewhat for granted. "I thought everyone had the governor and senator stay overnight in their house."

Now Bill describes himself as "a political gadfly" who works on fund-raising and other activities for Democrats, but who longs for a more responsible and responsive political climate in Wisconsin. "I think it's unfortunate that we demonize everybody," Bill laments. If you believe what you hear in today's political discourse, "the Democrats want to let rapists loose on the street, and Republicans want to push grandma off a cliff in a wheelchair. It's a good thing we aren't on opposite sides of the line," Bill remarks to me, "because Wisconsin is just brother against brother."*

The upcoming election will be just as divisive, Bill predicts, because the margins have become narrower. "We're fighting over 5 percent of the vote, maybe 7 percent of the vote—the people who can't make up their minds," he says, and this will make the fight both divisive and expensive. "We're going to spend how many millions of dollars trying to figure out who [those people] are."

That presents a problem for Democrats in 2016, because Barack Obama in 2008 was the kind of candidate who could step outside that paradigm and inspire casual voters to engage on a level not seen in more than forty years. "You saw a lot of young people around that you hadn't seen before," Bill says. "It was almost going back to the 1960s with Kennedy bringing in young people." That led not only to Obama's surprise victory in what Bill calls "small-C conservative Brown County" but also to the residual emotional connection that helped Obama to undercut Romney's challenge in 2012.

Obama "organized his own process," Bill says, and this could have "huge" implications in 2016. The Obama campaign bypassed the established party figures in building

---

* For this and other obvious reasons, Bill doesn't want his name to appear in this book. I have independently confirmed his authenticity.

their own organization, and local Democrats weren't much of a factor. The same held true for 2012, which means that the 2016 Democratic nominee must start from scratch when trying to duplicate Obama's success in the state.

The results of the recall and the 2014 gubernatorial election show that Democrats failed to do that, absent Obama on the ticket. Bill believes this reflects the quality of the candidate. "Scott Walker connects with them more than Romney, who looks like a really rich guy from the East Coast. At least with Obama there was the novelty factor," Bill says. "Some of us like to think, who understands my problems? Who understands that I have to buy gas, and I've got to buy groceries, and I've got to go to work? You can get some of that with Scott Walker."

But Bill feels that Wisconsin Democrats have one particular advantage in 2016 that hasn't attracted much attention: the Senate rematch between Russ Feingold and Ron Johnson. Johnson beat Feingold, a three-term incumbent, at the peak of the Tea Party movement for his first elected office. Six years later, the landscape looks different—but more important, Feingold has his operation "falling right back into place like it did six years ago."

Bill believes Johnson is not up for another dogfight. "You're going to have an extremely energetic Russ Feingold against a Ron Johnson who, from my observation, lacks fire in the belly this time."

But what about the presidential race? Hillary Clinton may not excite anyone like Obama did eight years earlier, but Bill thinks the campaign can make up for it in organization. "If she can get fifty-year-old women enthusiastic, that's what she's got to do, because they can rule the world," Bill says. "If you're talking about identity as somebody who understands my life, then she's had knocks personally; she's had knocks professionally. Most twenty-year-olds don't vote. But fifty- to sixty-year-olds do vote. I think that to prevail, she's going to have to make that connection."

Perhaps. But at least early in the primary campaign, Hillary Clinton didn't inspire much enthusiasm or confidence. Bernie Sanders packed arenas around the country, but he and most of the other Democratic Party hopefuls are well above sixty years of age—and Sanders and Joe Biden (who considered a challenge to Clinton but later passed) are both over seventy, and have been part of the Washington establishment for a long time. The "novelty factor" that Obama brought to the campaign, as Bill calls it, will not exist, and neither will the "Rorschach ink test" quality that allowed casual voters to project their own hopes onto the Democratic candidate.

Without Obama on the ticket, Democrats lost a half-million votes between 2012 and 2014. That gives Republicans an opening to find and inspire voters who may want a change after eight years.

CALLING THE RIGHT PLAYS

What issues will inspire voters in Brown County, those who want change and pragmatism?

Republicans may want to ask, at least as much as they ask for money. During one day, Tom Schmidt rejected half a dozen calls from the Republican Party hounding him for donations while he was working on his De Pere alpaca farm. When asked whether they ever came out to ask him what issues were important to him, Schmidt shook his head and said, "Never." He first moved to Brown County more than a decade ago, living at first in Bellevue, but never got any contact from the GOP there either except for donations. "In Bellevue, I never had anybody knocking at the door and asking me how I'm going to vote," Schmidt says.

Jerry Bader, who constantly takes the temperature of Brown County voters on his radio show, believes that national security and the economy will be the two issues that find the most resonance in the area. Government regulatory interference may be an especially effective area of economic policy, considering the county's major employers. "The paper industry continues to be critically important. Quite frankly, the toilet paper industry is still big," Bader says with a smile. "The most trouble that I ever got in with our mayor is . . . we were looking for a new city logo, and I said, *Toilet Paper Capital of the World. Your Crap Is Our Bread and Butter.*" Bader laughs. "I said that on the air. Oh, my God, he's still pissed about that."

Mark Graul links the county's industries to concerns over the Environmental Protection Agency. "This community was raised on paper mills, and the paper products industry is still one of the leading employers of the area," Graul says. "Everybody here understands that environmental extremism and paper mills don't go hand in hand." That gives the GOP nominee an opening to remind voters of how aggressively the EPA has behaved over the last several years under control of a Democratic White House. Graul says that a Republican arguing "I'm not trying to protect the giant corporate Wall Street guys, I'm trying to protect your job at the Fort Howard mill" will resonate with Brown County voters. "That's what they want to hear."

The challenge, Graul says, is to have a candidate who knows Brown County well enough to help voters connect the dots in a personal way. "Have somebody who can properly communicate what that means to the job at Schreiber Foods, or the job at Wisconsin Public Service, or the job at Sargento Cheese," Graul says. "If you start talking about the 111(d) rule or the Waters of America rule,* unless you're an insider on it, you're not going to know what you're talking about. Numbers mean nothing to people. What that means is specific jobs and specific communities."

Activists Jessika Olson and Jenn Jacques believe immigration "is going to be huge" in the 2016 election. Green Bay's expansion of low-income housing has pushed other voters out of the city into the suburbs, Jacques says, and it's creating another policy flash point. "[Green Bay mayor] Jim Schmidt opened Section 8 housing and said we want to diversify Green Bay, and made a bunch of changes after Hurricane Katrina," Jacques says, arguing that this led to a rise in crime and an influx of illegal immigrants who moved to the city for factory jobs.

---

* It's actually the Waters of the United States rule, which defines the jurisdiction of the EPA in enforcing the Clean Water Act. A number of states have challenged the most recent EPA interpretation. The 111(d) rule refers to the Clean Air Act, also enforced by the EPA. Graul's point is that talking about either without tying it to local issues will not be effective.

Graul believes immigration will be a "messy" issue in 2016, but that it might not break the way conservatives expect. This is due in part to the needs of the Green Bay industrial core, but also the dairy farms in the rural parts of Brown County. "You've got a dairy industry that would cease to exist without immigrants working on these dairy farms," he says. "You've got food processing industry, particularly the meat packing industry, that would have to shutter its doors without immigrant labor."

In Brown, the Republicans on the farms and the Democrats in the city may actually swap the traditional positions on immigration. The family farm has changed, and it takes outside labor to make it work. "You can't make it work anymore on thirty cows," Graul explains. "So farms are getting bigger to survive, and they're getting bigger and bigger. And they need workers on those farms, and they're not going to find that from white kids coming out of Bay Port High School. They're finding it in immigrant labor."

Ribble also warns about hitting immigration too hard in Brown County. "In Green Bay, there is an ever-growing Hispanic population. It certainly would not help anybody up there and in that entire market to take an anti-immigrant approach," Ribble advises. "That generally wouldn't work. Because just north of Green Bay and south of Green Bay are dairy farms, with a predominantly immigrant workforce."

It may not be about issues in Brown County as much as it is vision, Bader believes. "In 2010, Scott Walker defeated Tom Barrett because Barrett had no vision. Walker was very clear—*It's going this way*," Bader recalls. "State government is going to go this way: lower taxes, smaller government. There was a specific vision." A successful Republican candidate will answer two questions, Bader says: "What have you done, and what are you going to do?"

CHALK TALK

Scott Walker's success in winning two terms as governor, and beating a recall in between, serves as a marker for Republican success in Wisconsin. Not only did Walker win the office, he made significant and controversial changes, and then won again and kept the GOP's legislative majority in doing so. How did that happen? Walker himself spelled it out at the RedState Gathering in August 2015, in a meeting with Salem Media Group journalists and pundits.*

"Between 2012's recall and 2014's reelection, we spent four times more money on digital than we did two years ago," Walker explains when asked how he would approach the 2016 presidential election. "Why? Because when we contacted twice, we had twice as many personal contacts with voters in '14 as we did in '12. Even though we broke the record in '12 two years earlier."

Walker stresses that Obama's use of Facebook and other social media was not an end unto itself. "President Obama's big deal wasn't just that he used digital as though it was magically Facebook and Twitter," Walker says. "They used digital

---

* I write for HotAir.com, a property within the Salem Media Group, which employs me as senior editor and correspondent through its Townhall division.

to recruit and inform real people, who then talked to their neighbors. They talked to people they worked with. They talked to people they go to church with. The primary system is going to be driven by that," Walker predicts, "and so will the nominee" in the general election.

The other proven winner in Brown County and eastern Wisconsin, Reid Ribble, has advice for whoever wins the Republican nomination. "Genuineness and humility matters," he says. "There are some very traditional values that are held dearly in northeast Wisconsin, in Brown County, and genuineness and humility count," he emphasizes.

It's also important that the candidate demonstrate strength and dependability. "Show enough backbone so that you're going to be able to deal with the foreign affairs concerns and national security concerns that the Americans feel every day. When they see these terrorist attacks going on, when they see four marines and a sailor murdered by some terrorist in Chattanooga, Tennessee, that rattles them. Because that's a small town in America, so that could happen in Green Bay," Ribble says. "They want to sense that you're firm enough and strong enough on foreign policy that you're going to deal with those things."

RUNNING UP THE SCORE IN BROWN COUNTY

Wisconsin has been a reach for Republicans for more than thirty years. Even the addition of Paul Ryan to the ticket in 2012 didn't get Mitt Romney within 200,000 votes of winning the state.

But this doesn't mean Wisconsin shouldn't get attention in a Republican strategy for victory. Its congressional delegation includes five Republicans and three Democrats, demonstrating a competitiveness on the ground that has been lacking at the presidential level. Its ten Electoral College votes edge out more prominent swing states like Colorado (nine) and New Hampshire (four), both of which are featured in this book, and those ten electors may well make a difference in November 2016. Even if the GOP were to win back Florida, Virginia, Ohio, and New Hampshire from the Democrats in this cycle, they would fall eleven electors short of victory.

The bellwether quality of Brown County matters less from a win/lose perspective than in the depth of a victory. Lose it, and a Republican nominee has no chance at all of competing seriously; even a narrow victory would portend a significant defeat in the rest of the state. Bush won Brown by nine points and lost the state by one, so a win would have to be in double digits in Brown, at least. With a Feingold-Johnson rematch on the ballot, the GOP will have to vastly improve its ground game and its energy to deliver that kind of a rout.

A big win in Brown County, and a defeat of Democrats in the state, would show that Republicans have gained ground in the heart of the former "prairie populism" territory. It will force Democrats to play defense in this cycle and the cycles to come, eating up their resources. If the GOP ever wants to see its Wisconsin dream come true, this election gives them their best opportunity.

COLORADO

JEFFERSON COUNTY

BATTLEGROUND OF THE WEST

Jefferson County, Colorado, sits between the western border of Denver and the foothills of the Rocky Mountains. It is a true microcosm of American life—both culturally and geographically. As you drive through Jeffco, as locals call it, you embark on an elegant sweep through picturesque mountains and foothills before descending through rural, exurban, and suburban neighborhoods, all the way to the borders of the Mile High City. Coors beer, that most famous beverage of the Rocky Mountains, gets brewed in Golden, a town nestled into the mountains itself.

As one moves from east to west, and from north to south, the county becomes a study in contrasts. The western part of Jeffco is home to a unique blend of conservative conservationists and industry, while the eastern side of the county is in places almost indistinguishable from Denver. The northern end of Jeffco takes its cues more from Boulder, where many of the residents commute to work, and the central portion of the county, especially Lakewood, has a more working-class feel, with older strip malls and older homes (although both have recently begun to welcome newer and younger people from the Denver area).

It is because of this diversity that Jefferson County—and Colorado as a whole—has become a battleground between Republicans and Democrats, conservatives and progressives, and often between conservatives and Republicans. Barack Obama may have been the first Democrat since Franklin Delano Roosevelt to win the state twice, but the road to that victory started long before 2008.

FROM BASTION TO BATTLEGROUND

"I think with Jeffco Republicans, there was an arrogance that was born of decades of unchallenged success," says Rob Witwer, a Jeffco native who has worked in politics since his teens.

For many years, Jeffco and Colorado at large had been all but a lock for the GOP, especially in presidential elections. From the end of World War II until Barack Obama's first campaign, Colorado had gone to the Democrats in only three elections: 1948, 1964, and 1992, when baby boomers swept Bill Clinton to a national victory. But even Clinton couldn't create lasting momentum in the state, as Colorado would swing back to Bob Dole and the Republicans in 1996—an election that Clinton won decisively elsewhere in the country.

All of this began to change in the next decade, however, and the causes weren't entirely organic. In his book *The Blueprint*, coauthored with Adam Schrager, Witwer describes how deep-pocketed Democratic progressives took aim at the keystone of the Interior West and succeeded in painting it blue. In 2004, Colorado went to George W. Bush in the presidential race, but Democrats took control of both chambers of the state legislature, and the GOP lost the House seat in the 3rd Congressional District—a seat they had held for the previous twelve years.

In their book, Witwer and Schrager pinpoint the development that might have allowed Democrats an opening: a push by conservatives to enact term limits in the state legislature, which passed in 1990. Led by Republican state senator Terry Considine, the group Coloradans Back in Charge placed an initiative on the ballot that would limit officeholders to eight years. Their aim was to create a more responsive state government, one that would be run by citizen legislators and not professional politicians, and the initiative's success brought praise from high-profile conservative publications like *National Review.*

But the term-limit initiative also set the stage for a resurgent Democratic Party. "Democrats saw that a window of opportunity would open in 1998, the year the new law officially kicked in," Witwer and Schrager say.[1] With the power of incumbency broken down, Democrats had an opportunity for a fresh start throughout the state.

Shortly after those term limits went into effect, Jefferson County became one of the key battlegrounds in a fight that goes on to this day. In the 2000 cycle, Senate Minority Leader Mike Feely put together an alliance of progressive groups and unions to target seats usually easily held by Republicans. The AFL-CIO and the Colorado Education Association worked to unseat three Republican women in Jeffco, and Feely himself ended up winning control of the Colorado State Senate— the first Democrat to do so since John F. Kennedy was in the White House. Energized by the success of Feely's campaign,

Democrats began calling the 2000 election "the Colorado Miracle."

Republicans managed to win back control of the State Senate two years later, but in 2004, Democrats took control of both chambers. And by 2008, when Democrats chose to hold their national convention in Denver and nominate Barack Obama as their candidate, the progressive blueprint accomplished its goal of giving Democrats control of it all— the state legislature, the governorship, and Colorado's electoral votes in the national election.

What happened? Local politics plays a role in the story, as does internecine fighting among conservatives and Republicans in the face of a united Democratic-progressive front. But shifting demographics and the reemergence of a strong libertarian impulse have changed the landscape, too, and Republicans have yet to catch up. Neither of these trends will reverse themselves before the next election and likely will continue to accelerate. But if conservatives and Republicans are looking for a new way to win in this changing community, there are examples of success that they can follow.

TAKEOVER FROM THE LEFT

"When the demographics started to change underneath our feet," Witwer tells me, "we didn't roll up our sleeves and do the hard work of winning the voters over."

Colorado became a destination state in the 1990s, welcoming nearly one million migrants from the West and Midwest. As Witwer and Schrager note, the new arrivals "tended to be less rigid in their political affiliation," and their arrival began to shift the political winds in what had been a conservative stronghold.[2]

Today, Jefferson County is home to an estimated 558,000 people, with growth having slowed to single digits in the past decade. Demographically, Jeffco looks somewhat different from the rest of Colorado, in ways that arguably should benefit the Republican Party. Hispanic voters, however, form a significant part of the Jefferson County community. Fifteen percent of the population identifies as Hispanic, a lower percentage than the state (21%) or the United States as a whole (17.1%), but also up nearly a percentage point since 2010.

This increase may soon accelerate, according to Cameron Lynch of Compass Colorado. Gentrification in central Denver is causing Hispanic residents of the city to move west, into the eastern part of Jeffco. "West Denver was very Hispanic," Lynch explained, until a series of land use projects in the early 1990s centered on the closure of Lowry Air Force Base* made the city an attractive destination. This has dislocated traditionally Hispanic neighborhoods, whose residents have begun to see opportunities for home ownership in eastern

---

* The transition started with the Base Realignment and Closure (BRAC) program, which in 1991 targeted Lowry Air Force Base for closure. It became "the biggest internal land use project in the country," Lynch recalled, while at the same time Denver shut down its Stapleton International Airport and opened Denver International Airport outside the city. That opened another "huge chunk of land" for development, and both became remarkably homogeneous in demographics. "All the houses, all the development, all the shopping," Lynch says, "it's all white."

Jeffco, especially with reasonable housing costs in Lakewood, just to the west of Denver.

The population in Lakewood had already begun "graying out," as Lynch puts it. "And that's changing the political behavior of the county." It's no surprise, then, that in the 2004, 2008, and 2012 elections, it was in the eastern part of Jeffco that the Democrats found their biggest gains.

How, then, can Republicans gain traction with Hispanic voters in Jefferson County, whether those voters are transitioning from Denver or are more rooted in Jeffco? State representative Jon Keyser, who won his district in the western half of Jefferson County in 2014, says that the key to winning here is getting to know the voters rather than assessing them based on assumption.

"I hope that we don't have presidential candidates that come to Jeffco and just want to talk about illegal immigration," Keyser says. Single-issue campaigning wouldn't appeal to Hispanics anywhere, Keyser advises, but particularly not in Jefferson County.

"I did a radio interview in Spanish," Keyser recalls, and one caller wanted to hear the candidate's position on the use of private security forces such as Blackhawk as part of national security policy. "I didn't get a question about immigration . . . the Hispanic community cares a lot about all kinds of different issues." Just as with Keyser's other voters, the Hispanic community has deep concerns about what he calls "the four Es": the economy and education in particular, but also energy and the environment.

If Republicans want to learn how to campaign effectively in the Hispanic community, Keyser suggests they study how

Mike Coffman succeeded. After winning his first two congressional elections easily, with more than 60% of the vote both times, Coffman found himself in a dogfight in 2012. Having Barack Obama at the top of the ticket made Coffman's plight even more acute. He barely survived, beating his challenger by a slim 47/45 margin.

Up for reelection in 2014, Coffman knew he had to change his approach. Instead of relying on a base-turnout strategy, Coffman became "very active in the [Hispanic] community," Keyser recalls, while Democrats just assumed that the same voters would go with the Democrats. Coffman "took it upon himself to learn Spanish," hoping to compete with his opponent, a fluent Spanish speaker. And he didn't just memorize a handful of token sentences, either: Coffman learned the language well enough to agree to a Spanish-language debate.

"Did Congressman Coffman speak perfect Spanish?" Keyser says. "Definitely not. But I think he showed that conservative values in many cases are consistent with values in the Hispanic community and the Latino community. And I think he showed that he cared, and that is something that transcends ethnicity, race, and anything else."

Kelly Maher of Compass Colorado was amazed at Coffman's effort. "If somebody had told me ten years ago that Mike Coffman would be running in Tom Tancredo's old district and would do a debate with his opponent on Univision in Spanish," Maher says, laughing, "I would have said, 'You have lost your damn mind.'" Coffman "did it right" by doing it himself, Maher stresses. Many Republicans, both candidates and organizations, try taking a shortcut by "hiring a brown person with a Hispanic surname," a kind of tokenism that is not only "hugely ineffective," but also offensive.

Daniel Garza of the LIBRE Initiative offers a different perspective on outreach. "We've always believed that there is no silver bullet to advance your ideas, and it has to be a comprehensive strategy, and it has to be very local, very localized," he says, "and the priority issues are the ones that matter to different individuals in different communities."

In Colorado, Garza believes that the Hispanic vote can be won—or at least made competitive—as soon as Republicans grasp this. "Barack Obama got 59 percent of the Latino vote in 2008, and people said, 'God, it couldn't get any worse,'" Garza recalls. "But it did. He got 80 percent of the vote in 2012 in Colorado." Two years later, though, that changed, thanks to the adept campaign of Cory Gardner in the Senate race (and perhaps the ineptitude of incumbent Mark Udall). "Cory Gardner got 45 percent of the vote," Garza points out. Smart engagement may not *win* the Hispanic vote in the short term, but Gardner's success shows that Republicans can compete when they make the effort to do so.

At the same time, Republicans need to craft a message that speaks to the community's concerns on economic growth and improved education. Mastering that message will require effort by the GOP to make themselves part of the lives of these voters. "The candidate has to hire folks on their staff that look like us and speak like us, who have a shared language," Garza continues. "Getting past the noise and getting your message and your ideas out to people. I think Gardner did that very well—and Udall took him for granted."

Republicans cannot count on that happening again, which makes these lessons all the more imperative. The GOP has missed out on opportunities to make inroads in a fast-growing demographic in the American electorate. They need to start reversing that soon, or face dire consequences in future elections. And the longer Republicans wait, the more difficult it will become.

THE BIGGEST OF THE BIG ES

Thanks to its relatively recent growth spurt, there aren't too many parts of Jeffco that seem old or worn-out—but neither does the county appear conspicuously affluent. A drive through Lakewood, one of Jeffco's working-class communities, reveals an area that looks similar to other older suburban centers: solid, serviceable, if unspectacular.

One exception to that rule can be found on Colfax Avenue, one of the main thoroughfares that take residents into Denver. In the middle of an otherwise unremarkable retail strip mall, a giant pink spire ascends above the architecture, announcing the presence of the legendary family entertainment center, Casa Bonita. Once featured as a plotline in the libertarian-tinged animated TV series *South Park*, Casa Bonita has been a fixture in Jefferson County and the greater Denver area for more than forty years. With a vaudeville show that features acrobats diving off cliffs in the center of the restaurant, two or more generations of children throughout the greater Denver metropolitan area have grown up coming here for birthday parties and other festivities.

Even with its otherwise modest trappings, Jeffco's economy significantly outpaces the state as a whole (and the state actually outpaces the United States). After the Great Recession, the median household income in the United States has rebounded upward to $53,046,[3] but Colorado's median household income is more than 10% better, at $58,433. In Jeffco, household income as of 2013 reached $68,984, 18% higher than Colorado's median and 30% higher than the national median.

The rural areas in the western part of the county—as well as those at the northern end, which serve as bedroom communities to Boulder and Denver—are solidly upper middle class. The areas where Denver residents have migrated into Jeffco, which tend to be more working class, are at the eastern edge and center of the county—places like Wheat Ridge, Lakeside, and Lakewood. The West Colfax neighborhood, where Casa Bonita operates, is one of the few lower-income areas in Jefferson County.

Despite this mix of income levels, poverty does not weigh on Jeffco like it does in other first-ring suburban counties throughout the United States. Only 9.1% of Jefferson County residents live below the poverty line, compared with 13% in Colorado and 14.5% nationally. Jeffco holds 10.4% of Colorado's population, but 11.3% of its businesses and 11.7% of its businesses are owned by women. While population growth has plateaued over the last several years, economic growth has kept pace and, in fact, expanded in Jeffco.

Unsurprisingly, voters in Jefferson County remained focused on economic issues more than others when it comes to determining their vote. State Representative Jon Keyser insists that an economic agenda remains key to any hopes of connecting with voters in his district, emphasizing again the "four Es" as the key to all Jeffco voters. What won't win votes, Keyser says, are the traditional social issues. "Social issues come up rarely with unaffiliated voters," Keyser says, "and even with Republicans." Social conservatives aren't unknown in Jeffco by any means, but they also tend to prioritize the economic and free-market issues.

Energy and economy combine with free-market principles for Craig Hunsicker, a millennial Jeffco voter from the eastern part of the county. He lives in newer developments practically on the doorstep of the foothills, where tech companies and industry have built campuses to attract cutting-edge talent. Housing tracts have sprawled out from the eastern portion of the county in patchwork fashion, with large gaps of undeveloped land between them. Hunsicker and his wife occasionally worry about urban sprawl into the west, but for now, "it's a great place to move to."

Hunsicker describes the political environment as being libertarian, but inclined toward fiscal conservatism. Social issues tend to strike him and his friends as "nanny state" impositions; but their perception is that, while Republicans drive those issues too much as candidates, Democrats are the ones who actually impose those kinds of laws in office.

A recent fight over fracking in Colorado helped clarify this point, Hunsicker explains. Democratic governor John Hickenlooper tried pushing more regulations on fracking in 2014, starting a fight that nearly cost him a second term in November. Younger voters bristled at the intrusion, seeing it as a threat to a potential economic boon. "It's that kind of governmental encroachment on people, on business, that is just not impressing Coloradans," Hunsicker says. "That's something that [could] really make inroads for a Republican candidate here."

However, Hunsicker has a healthy amount of skepticism for politicians who promise to create jobs, even when those politicians are fiscal conservatives. "People around here are pretty confident that they can produce their own jobs and drive their own economy," he explains, "if the government will get out of the way."

Alan Philp, who once served as the executive director of the Colorado Republican Party, sees the same trend. Jeffco, he says, is "libertarian on the social issues, but on fiscal economics issues, it's wired to be pretty conservative." That may not be as true for the northeastern end of the county, where the majority of the flip occurred for Barack Obama in 2008 and 2012, thanks to its economic and cultural connections to the deep-blue city of Boulder. Philp notes that "the Boulder mind-set"—more progressive, more activist, and certainly more a part of the Obama coalition—projects "into Westminster . . . a little bit into northern Jeffco."

Even there, though, the prevailing culture should favor fiscal conservatives if they stick to limited-government principles. "If I had to point to a message that I think would uniquely suit your average independent Jefferson County voter," Philp advises, " 'leave us alone' is the message that politicians should give. People are looking for leaders who are going to get the government out of the way, whether it's on social, economic, fiscal policy, or whatever."

Philp sees an opportunity for Republicans if they push

for meaningful tax reform in 2016. The middle-class community in Jeffco has hearkened to Democratic arguments that the tax code is unfair, so "why don't we go ahead and take and run with that type of message?" Philp asks. Point out the "corporate welfare and these tax carve-outs, and so forth," he says. "Come out in opposition to some of the more egregious examples, and talk about a fairer and flatter tax code." That would not only appeal to the leave-us-alone spirit of Jeffco, Philp says; it would provide a meaningful rebuttal to the Democratic economic argument, which relies on *more* government intervention.

Rob Witwer concurs but warns that merely discussing proposals isn't going to be enough. Part of the trouble Republicans have had in Jeffco is that they've talked past and around voters, spouting ideological and philosophical arguments that fail to relate to them in a personal way. "Republicans will do better when they can find a way to connect the dots between our philosophical beliefs, which are sound," Witwer explains, "and then draw a direct connection to the life experience of the people whose votes we're trying to win."

It's that last part that Republicans have not yet learned, Witwer laments. "To this day, Republicans in Jefferson County do not feel the obligation to directly communicate to constituents, which is a huge [mistake]," he says. Republicans have to "understand the day-to-day experience of voters as a way of communicating our core principles to them." Instead, they believe that all they need do is say, " 'These are my core principles. This is what I stand for. That should be all I need to do.' It's not enough. You have to do the hard work of explaining why those principles should also be important to that voter." Witwer adds, "Democrats do a terrific job of that."

As a former state legislator from Jefferson County, Cheri Gerou has seen this performance gap up close. Democrats had better technology to apply to their get-out-the-vote effort, but they also connected with voters on a much more personal level. "They would record if they came to your door and you complained about the trash service or whatever, they would input those data," Gerou recounts. "The next time somebody came to your door, they would say that well, we understand that you really weren't happy about the trash service, so we were talking about doing blah-blah-blah."

Republicans struggled in comparison, a shortcoming Gerou experienced before she ran for office. While working as a volunteer, one candidate shrugged off the idea of reaching out to Republican voters. " 'Well, I'm not going to spend any money on any Republican mailings, because they're just going to automatically vote for me,' " Gerou recalls the candidate telling her. "And I remember thinking to myself, 'Wow, you really think so? You think you don't need to do any wooing at all, or even a Thank you, here I am, I'm a resource for you if you need me'? They were just completely ignoring Republican voters."

The party didn't do enough to boost a sense of identity, either. The GOP appeared stuck between the inertia of their previous dominance in Jeffco and the change in emphasis among the transitioning demographics in the county. That left Republicans somewhat unsure of who they were in Jeffco's new environment. "If they could have done something to help the Republican voters feel like they were proud to be Republican in Jefferson County," Gerou says, "I think that would have helped the cause, but that never happened. Never happened."

The problem has been chronic, says Cameron Lynch at Compass Colorado. Democrats do field research that tells them who voters actually are and what issues drive their decisions; but the GOP's field research focuses mainly on candidates and the context of an upcoming election. "[Democrats have] kids sitting down here in the 16th Street Mall, four blocks from here, with a clipboard, attacking anybody who walks in front of them, saying, 'Do you have a minute for the environment?' And everybody who signs up gets put on an environmental voter list, which is appended to everything the Democrats ever do," Lynch says. "And then suddenly you're going to get e-mails saying Cameron Lynch hates the environment. Hates it. Wants to burn it down. And asphalt over it. Because that's a value question that has long-term significance to people and will transcend whether the individual candidate is Mitt Romney or Barack Obama," he explains. "We never ask that."

Voter-based research has empowered Democrats to fight Republicans and turn Jeffco into a battleground county. But Jeffco has turned into a battleground of another sort, too— one that pits Republicans against Republicans.

JEFFCO'S "BIBLE BELT," AND INTERNECINE WARFARE

In 2004, the flip in Jeffco took place mainly in the northeastern corner of the county, in the more densely populated cities of Westminster and Arvada. Those two cities form part of the first ring of suburbs around Denver, but they also serve as bedroom communities for Boulder, a hub of progressive politics and high-tech industry.

Despite the sway of progressive politics in this corner of Jefferson County, it still seems surprising that the shift here was so strong. The neighborhoods in these areas tend more toward the upper middle class, which means that these are neighborhoods in which conservative fiscal policy should find a foothold, and there's a religious streak here that should play to Republicans' favor. Lynn Bartels, who worked as a reporter for the *Rocky Mountain News* and the *Denver Post* from 1993 until taking a position in mid-2015 as communications director for Secretary of State Wayne Williams,[4] calls northeastern Jeffco a kind of "Bible Belt."

A handful of megachurches have built large congregations in the area. "When you have churches that have to have cops on the weekend because you've got that big of a turnout," Bartels notes, "it makes a difference." However, Bartels cautions that people in these areas are "not necessarily wanting a right-winger." They draw their congregations not just from the more conservative areas of Jeffco, but also from its working-class neighborhoods.

Norma Anderson, the first woman ever to serve in the State House, says that the "Bible Belt" appellation applies mainly to one particular megachurch in Arvada, which has grown so large that a walkway was built to allow pedestrians to move across a busy street that runs through its campus. Its congregation tends to push for doctrinaire candidates, along with other conservatives in the area, but they don't have the strength to succeed in electing them. This, Anderson says, tends to turn off unaffiliated voters, who then decide to "vote with the Democrats."

The tension between fiscal and social conservatism in Jeffco is palpable, and Anderson says that this isn't all due to the "Bible Belt" in Arvada. She blames Dudley Brown,* founder of Rocky Mountain Gun Owners and a conservative activist who has sparred with the National Rifle Association for being too accommodating on gun rights.†

Brown's influence on elections is not limited to gun issues. One activist who preferred to remain unnamed recalled that Brown distributed mailers in several Colorado primaries that accused Republican candidates of being soft on same-sex marriage. The mailer featured a picture of two men kissing, a picture reportedly taken from a same-sex wedding in New York City. "[Brown] raises money from gun people,"

---

* I reached out to Dudley Brown through RMGO for comment, but did not get a response. I did, however, end up on their e-mail distribution list.

† Thanks to a national effort to push gun magazine capacity restrictions after the Newtown shooting, the Democrat-controlled legislature passed a law restricting magazine capacities for semiautomatic firearms to ten rounds. A recall of two state legislators—with significant work done by Brown and RMGO—and a shift in control of the legislature gave conservatives an opportunity to raise the capacity to thirty rounds, which would exceed the needs of most gun owners, but Brown wanted the limit raised to fifty. "Dudley Brown told every one of those legislators, even the sponsor of the bill, that he would go after them in a primary if they didn't kill that bill," Anderson recalled. "They killed it because it wasn't fifty."

one activist noted, "and turns around and spends it on gay marriage–civil union" issues.

Others, who preferred not to go on the record, aired frustration with Brown and the way he uses his power to attack fellow Republicans. Those who did comment accuse Brown of playing a dog-in-the-manger role, spending money not to achieve electoral success, but to punish would-be allies for failing to adopt his agenda in toto.

However, not everyone agrees with that assessment. Best-selling author and longtime conservative firebrand Michelle Malkin* considers the complaints against Brown to be a case of sour grapes from the moderate wing of the party. "Dudley is definitely a mover, shaker, and disruptor here in Colorado," the Fox News contributor explained in an e-mail. "I like him because he keeps the state GOP establishment on its toes."

Nor has Brown contented himself to merely play spoiler. The Denver magazine *5280*[5] noted the day after the midterm elections that three of his endorsed candidates won their legislative elections. Those victories "deflat[ed] the notion that Brown sponsors candidates who are too extreme to win a statewide race," wrote Luc Hatlestad. "In fact, the Colorado GOP will now hold an advantage in the State Senate next term, and it also narrowed its deficit in the House."

All of this may seem like "inside baseball" to outsiders.

---

* Full disclosure: Michelle Malkin is a longtime friend of mine, as well as my employer for two years until she and her husband, Jesse, sold HotAir.com in February 2010 to Salem Media Group, my current employer.

But it's important to note because, in order to win in Jeffco and Colorado, the GOP nominee will need to successfully navigate this conflict among Republicans and conservatives in the state. The antipathy between conservative activists and what they see as an unresponsive Republican establishment has played out nationally, too—most recently in the fight over congressional leadership that ended up with House Speaker John Boehner's resignation.

A campaign that fails to learn this political topography and engage the players in a way that encourages passionate voters to show up at the polls will find itself on the losing end. And if this happens in Jeffco, it could prove disastrous for the national hopes of Republicans.

CONSERVATIONIST CONSERVATIVES

On the other end of the right-leaning spectrum, Jeffco conservatism has one quality that makes it unique among battleground counties: a strong bent toward conservation- ism. Conservationism and environmentalism are tradition- ally hallmarks of the liberal side of the American political spectrum, but in Jeffco, where a majestic sweep of the Rocky Mountains forms a backdrop in the west, conservationism is a powerful force across the political spectrum. Former *Denver Post* reporter Lynn Bartels notes that "out in the mountains, [voters] tend to be more conservative, but they're enviros."

Jon Keyser warns that people move to Colorado or stay in the state in significant part because of its natural beauty, so Republicans running national messaging that disparages environmentalism could experience backfire in Jeffco. "It's a different brand of Republican," Keyser says, describing his constituents in western Jefferson County. "As a Colorado native, I think of myself more as a preservationist or a conservationist than as an environmentalist. I think that's true for a lot of the people in the district as well." He pledged to voters in his strongly Republican State House district to "preserve Colorado for future generations. . . . I want my kids and the kids that are in my district to certainly be able to grow up and enjoy Colorado for what it is."

The alternative for Jeffco voters, Keyser explains, becomes all too clear when they drive into Denver for their morning commutes. "When we come into work, we see brown clouds hanging over Denver, and we're just like *yuck*. That's what we're going to go breathe all day. It's a tangible pollution that you can see."

Witwer says Democrats have used these environmental concerns to convert Jeffco voters, beginning in the 1990s. "Democrats got very shrewd about speaking directly to voters about issues that matter to voters," he says, echoing Lynch. "They targeted women in Jeffco around issues of health care, education, and environment. Those issues were very important to those voters. . . . They're talking about the environment in your backyard." By contrast, Republicans began focusing on social conservatism, rather than presenting their own agenda based on what mattered most to people who call Jeffco home.

This presents a challenge for the GOP, as they think about how to turn out Republicans while also wooing independents. How do they balance limited-government principles with the need to address environmental preservation? Fortunately, the Obama administration has unintentionally handed the GOP a ready-made argument that aggressive government intervention does not necessarily mean *conservation.*

In August 2015, the Environmental Protection Agency accidentally breached a dam that had quarantined heavily contaminated water at old mining sites from the Animas River.[6] Three million gallons of contaminated water flowed into the Animas in La Plata County, near the New Mexico border, creating an environmental catastrophe. The EPA dragged its feet in explaining what had happened; meanwhile, the toxic river ran into the San Juan River, and tests a week later showed "lead levels more than 200 times the acute exposure limit for aquatic life and more than 3,500 times the limit for human ingestion," according to CBS News.[7]

The response from Governor John Hickenlooper exacerbated the impression of incompetence. In a poorly advised stunt,[8] Hickenlooper tried drinking from the now-orange river after treating it with an iodine tablet in order to prove it was safe. Coloradans could clearly see the toxic sludge had not abated, and testing proved that it was dangerous. The impression was that Democrats wanted to rally to protect the EPA rather than the environment.

New Mexico's Environment Department secretary Ryan Flynn not only blasted the EPA for delaying notification of the spill, but also Hickenlooper for his dangerous stunt. "If it's true, it's a reckless and irresponsible act by a public official," Flynn said.[9] "He might as well stick fifteen cigarettes in his mouth, light them all at the same time, and take a picture to show how that's good for you."

In this election cycle, the EPA and the Democratic governor will find themselves on the defensive. La Plata residents worry that the EPA has killed their tourism industry, and some now wonder whether the EPA may have deliberately created the catastrophe in order to push Superfund status[10] on the mine sites in La Plata, wresting even more control from local and state officials. If nothing else, the disaster has made the longtime joke "We're from the government and we're here to help" even more bitterly ironic.

In 2016, Republicans will have an opening to produce a plan that curtails government intrusion on use of private land, while leveraging local controls rather than federal power to preserve the natural beauty of Colorado. The presidential campaign would be wise to speak with Jeffco voters—and especially successful officeholders like Keyser, Anderson, and Gerou—to strategize for success.

MILE HIGH: THE MARIJUANA DEBATE

In November 2012, Colorado and Washington became the first two states in the United States to legalize recreational marijuana use, although other states had allowed marijuana sales for medicinal use. In June 2015, the state reported that monthly marijuana sales exceeded $50 million,[11] with licensed dispensaries having been opened all over the state. In the first six months of 2015, Colorado took in more than $60 million in taxes and fees from the marijuana industry, corroborating the argument that legalization would bring a boon to the state's economy.

For Coloradans, marijuana legalization is a settled issue, fitting neatly with the "leave us alone" ethos described above. "It didn't really figure into the Senate campaign with Gardner and Udall," Independence Institute political analyst Ben DeGrow says.

Kelly Maher sees the legalization initiative as a success in the American tradition of allowing states to be laboratories of democracy. "We're always a couple years ahead of people in terms of what issue is about to come up," Maher says. "Whether it's gun control or marijuana, [Colorado is] the place where people like to message-test."

In 2016, at least five states will put measures on their ballots legalizing marijuana.[12] A Republican presidential nominee may not have much chance of winning California or Massachusetts, but they will need to win in Nevada and Arizona, and they'll need to at least compete in Maine. Hewing too much to a socially conservative, antilegalization line will impact a candidate's ability to compete not only in Jeffco and Colorado, but also in other states where younger voters and more libertarian-minded independents will be motivated to get to the polling stations.

Philp's advice should be well taken by the Republican nominee: *leave us alone.* Or, at the very least, endorse the federalist approach.

GOING RED IN THE ROCKY MOUNTAIN STATE

Everyone agrees that Jeffco is the bellwether county for Colorado, but many believe that Republicans will need to stretch if they want to win it in 2016. "It's become more of a bellwether" than in the days of Republican domination, says Alan Philp, but "maybe even a twitch toward Democrats on the overall scheme of things."

Jefferson County is the kind of community where Republicans *should* do well. They have a stronger and more consistent commitment to limited government, while the Democratic Party's support comes from progressives who support regulation and big-government solutions. The difficulties of ethnic demographics in some other battlegrounds are less urgent in Jefferson County, and residents' relative affluence should provide friendly turf for conservatives' free-market economic policies.

In other words, Republicans can find a friendly constituency here in 2016—if they learn to engage residents on the issues that *they* care about. Keyser's "four Es"—economy, education, energy, and the environment—provide the best opportunities for turning out their base and attracting independents, which is the key to winning Jeffco. But thus far, Republicans have yet to find the right formula.

Although the GOP competed better in Jeffco in 2014, they hardly got a full-throated endorsement from voters. Governor John Hickenlooper won Jeffco by almost six points in his successful reelection bid, a margin that was twice what he got in the rest of the state.[13] Cory Gardner unseated incumbent Senator Mark Udall by almost 50,000 votes statewide and two and a half percentage points, but won Jeffco by just 120 votes.

The Republican coalition in Jeffco—and Colorado at large—exhibit the same factions seen at the national level: tensions between libertarians and social conservatives, grassroots activists and pragmatic office-seekers, and the added layer of conservationists who may be turned off by a national GOP message against extreme environmentalism. To win in 2016, the Republican nominee must navigate those divisions carefully at the national level, and Jeffco will provide a bellwether of success in that effort. Alan Philp's "leave us alone" approach will have a lot of appeal across those lines, and the misadventures of the EPA in Colorado gave the GOP a huge gift that Republicans cannot afford to squander.

Republicans will have an uphill fight to reclaim Jeffco, but it can be done. The GOP and conservative activists have to take a page from Coffman and Keyser to expand the reach of the GOP into Jeffco's growth communities, but also to get their own house in order. Provide a realistic, pragmatic, and conservative approach to governance, Keyser says, and Jeffco will respond.

"Colorado has an independent streak. My district has an independent streak. People care generally more about good public policy than they do about the letter after a politician's name," Keyser says. "They'll be looking for someone who they can identify as not necessarily being postpartisan, but someone who isn't going to be completely beholden to a party and someone who can transcend the R or the D a little bit. Someone with a persona and a platform that is inclusive, that is accepting, that people can get excited about."

As both Keyser and Coffman discovered in their own campaigns, that is a recipe for success in Jeffco and Colorado. And it just might have appeal beyond those lines, as well.

NEW HAMPSHIRE

HILLSBOROUGH COUNTY
ALL POLITICS IS LOCAL

There is no small irony to the outsized role that New Hampshire plays in national politics. Although the Granite State only ranks forty-second in population, with just over 1.32 million residents, it occupies the first position in the presidential primaries of both major parties. The Iowa caucuses take place at an earlier date but are not binding, so New Hampshire's primaries provide the first delegate commitments for presidential contenders, giving a significant boost in stature to the winner. Even in the general election, in which New Hampshire holds only four Electoral College votes, its results are considered a cue for whether a candidate can succeed in wooing independents.

The old aphorism "all politics is local" is nowhere more true than in New Hampshire. The state's bicameral legislature has 424 members, making it the fourth-largest English-speaking legislative body in the world (behind Congress and the parliaments of India and the United Kingdom).[1] Legislators receive only $100 per year in salary, plus a per diem for each day the legislature is in session, and Milford town moderator Pete Basiliere points out that this impacts who runs for office. A typical candidate "is a successful businessman who can get away, or someone who is retired," Basiliere says. "Both of those tend to lean fiscally conservative." The upside for Basiliere is that "there are no professional politicians" in the legislature, and that representatives feel accountable to their constituents.

As they should, given the math. Each member in the State House represents approximately 3,315 New Hampshire residents. By contrast, neighboring Massachusetts, which ranked fourteenth among states for population, has one member in its House for every 40,875 residents.*

An attachment to local control runs "deep in the DNA of this state," says Milford attorney David Sturm. "New Hampshire has very limited government," he explains, "and things tend to be pushed down to the local level." Volunteers fill roles that in other states would be filled by paid officials; Sturm himself serves as "a cemetery trustee, a school district moderator, and town moderator."

"We still have town meetings where we all get together on a Tuesday night or a Saturday," Sturm says. "We debate. Vote on things right there, right then."

Patrick Hynes, a political consultant, recalls how politicians used to go into a Milford coffee shop to shake a few hands, only to get more than they bargained for. "They keep a copy of the budget in the coffee shop," Hynes says, "and when politicians go in there and try to do the handshaking thing, they will bust it out and get into a fight with them

---

* It's even more local than local government. Manchester has fourteen aldermen to represent its population of slightly over 110,000 people, which equates to one alderman for every 7,885 residents.

about it." The coffee shop recently closed, Hynes later noted, but residents' keen interest in the granular details of policy remains unabated.

The result of such local control over politics is a very informed and active citizenry—and this is nowhere more true than it is in Hillsborough County, the state's main prize.

INDEPENDENT THINKERS—AND VOTERS

Almost a third of New Hampshire's residents live in Hillsborough County, making it northern New England's most populous county. Hillsborough dates back to the colonial era, when King George III granted approval for its founding in March 1771. Hillsborough was originally one of five counties created to make New Hampshire more practical to govern. Its the current boundaries were drawn in 1823, when thirteen towns split off to form neighboring Merrimack.

In this split, Hillsborough lost 30% of its population,[2] but within twenty years, population growth had pushed Hillsborough above its previous peak. The county's most sustained period of growth came between 1960 and 1990, when each of the three decades showed over 20% growth, and population rose by 88.6% combined. Patrick Hynes chalks up that growth to "tax refugees" from neighboring states. "During that time, most Northeast states engaged in a decades-long experiment with government expansion and the resulting necessary tax increases," he says. "Overtaxing income and sales drove tens of thousands of families to New Hampshire."

Hillsborough has plenty of small business to sustain it, but also a couple of major employers. "Anheuser-Busch has a fairly large brewery in the Manchester area," New Hampshire's deputy secretary of state Dave Scanlan points out, and "some large technical and aerospace firms down in the Nashua area," whose names keep changing, Scanlan notes.

Demographically, the state of New Hampshire is much more homogeneous than the United States, and Hillsborough County only slightly less so. African Americans make up 13.2% of the US population, but only 1.5% of New Hampshire, and just 2.6% of Hillsborough. Whereas blacks outnumber Asians by more than double in the United States (5.3%), Asians outnumber blacks in both the state (2.4%) and county (3.6%) populations. Hispanics comprise a larger share than either, at 3.2% for New Hampshire and 5.8% in Hillsborough.

Even after all that growth in the second half of the last century, not much has changed except the numbers. "Ultimately," says Hynes, "this is still New Hampshire the way it looked thirty, forty years ago—mostly white, mostly middle class to upper middle class in some of those communities." Economically, Hillsborough outperforms the United States and New Hampshire on most measures. Median household income in 2013 was almost $70,000, 31.6% higher than the national average of $53,046, and the level of poverty (9.3%) was significantly lower than the national average as well (14.3%). The labor force participation rate outpaced that of the United States, 71.4% to 63.8%.

"Our tax-friendly environment has certainly encouraged

a lot of folks to move up here, which is wonderful," says Jayne Millerick, former chair of the Republican State Committee. Others come for "our beautiful mountains and lakes." This, Millerick says, has begun to change the dynamic of New Hampshire's traditional limited-government politics. "The challenge is that the states that they're coming from are states that are definitely states that enjoy a lot of government benefits."

This may explain some of the recent difficulties that Republicans have faced in New Hampshire, but it doesn't explain them *all*. For the moment, the GOP easily controls the state legislature, holding 239 seats of the 400 in the House, and 14 of the 24 seats in the State Senate. But that may be misleading, too. The strength of the state's political environment belongs to independents (formally known as "undeclared"), and they drive elections.

"Undeclared" docsn't necessarily equate to moderate or centrist, and certainly doesn't mean disinterested, at least not in New Hampshire. Steve Sareault identifies as a conservative, for instance, but he stays registered as an independent. "I don't like either party to take advantage of me," he says, a common theme among voters in the Granite State.

Scanlan says that this has created an interesting dynamic in New Hampshire's politics. The state had remained reliably Republican at all levels until the end of the large growth cycle in the postwar period, when towns and cities took on a more Democratic makeup and the political environment became more polarized. "We started seeing some huge swings in terms of the makeup of the state legislature," Scanlan explains.

This back-and-forth dynamic makes sense when one considers how independents are likely to react to a polarized political environment. "That block of undeclared voters gets simply fed up with the policies of the party in power," Scanlan says. "They throw them out en masse by voting for candidates of the other party, regardless of what the individuals may stand for. It's just cleaning house, and seeing if we can do better."

The Sturms are examples of this independent streak. Both attorneys and both active in their community of Milford, the husband-and-wife team hold opinions and voting records that don't fit neatly into either party's paradigms. David voted for Ronald Reagan twice and George H. W. Bush once but has voted for Democratic presidential nominees ever since. Sheila Sturm voted for George W. Bush in 2000, saying "that was Al Gore's fault. I don't think he really wanted it." Sheila voted for Obama in both 2008 and 2012.

While neither of the Sturms would fit the common profile of Republican voters, they do have a track record of at least being open to the GOP. That said, both say a Republican vote in the 2016 election is a long shot, mainly because of the tone of the campaigns. "They're appealing too much to the base," David says, although "the primary system is to blame for that. Too many of them are playing too hard to the primary base."

Sheila puts it more succinctly—and colorfully. When asked why she, and Hillsborough County at large, shifted away from the GOP, she replies, "The first thing that comes to mind to answer that question is Tea Partiers, and, excuse my language, but crazy bat-shit Republicans." Sheila is less concerned with the candidates than with "the people you see in the news, the people that are making the headlines, the people that are screaming the loudest." As a self-professed moderate, Sheila says, "I'm not hearing any moderate message from the Republican Party. I'm staying over here by the Democrat side, because it's safe over here."

What kind of focus could entice the Sturms to return? For both Sheila and David, a focus on tolerance would be a start. Sheila hears it from her Republican friends but doesn't see it emphasized in GOP campaigns. "I feel like I get the message from them that it's us or them, and it's not all of us."

David wants to see more of a commitment to a libertarian approach on social issues. "I'm very much into social libertarianism. That's where conservatism has it wrong," he says. "A truly conservative person would look at a lot of issues and just say I've got no business with that. I don't care. Do what you want."

"I care about the social issues," says Sareault, who identifies more with Republicans, but "I don't vote on the social issues." He tends to agree with David on emphasis, arguing that Republican infighting on social issues allows "Democrats [to] define the Republican Party rather than the Republican Party defining themselves. Then mass media walks onto it and drives it that way."

The infighting among Republicans turns off Basiliere, too. Basiliere is now an independent, but at one time he was an active member of the Republican Party in Hillsborough, participating in voter drives and get-out-the-vote efforts. "But when the Republicans started calling each other by the four letter word, RINO [Republican in name only], I just got . . . you know," he explains with a shrug. "It's that kind of attitude that's still present. If you don't come to the party line, and the far-right party line, then you're not a Republican."

In fact, Basiliere's personal voting pattern mirrors the recent history of Hillsborough County in presidential elections. He voted for George Bush in 2004, and for Barack Obama in the next two elections. "I just believed that he was going to be able to make a change," Basiliere recalls, although the straw that broke the camel's back for him was John McCain's selection of Sarah Palin as his running mate. Mainly, though, he saw McCain as being too embedded in the Washington, DC, establishment to enact reform, and Obama offered a chance at something new.

Four years later, Basiliere didn't see another option, especially with Mitt Romney's notorious remark about "the 47 percent." But that "was just one of numerous reasons," Basiliere said. "His constant flip-flopping . . . he was just too much with the wind in the Republican Party."

Like with the Sturms, Basiliere might be difficult to woo back in 2016. "Right now, I'm leaning Democrat," he says.

The good news for Republicans is that other independents in New Hampshire want a change in direction, the kind that they've imposed on the state legislative elections in the past. Jeanine Soffran has a unique history among Hillsborough voters I met—she voted for John McCain in 2008, but Obama in 2012. Her husband did the same. "There wasn't any one specific thing that made me change," Soffran says about her decision to vote for Obama's reelection. "I wanted to get behind the presidency where it was going, and I felt like my vote was better suited in that direction."

In 2016, Soffran is ready to return to the Republican

banner, although she firmly remains undeclared in her registration. "In a general, broad sense," she says, "a Republican in the White House is imperative after the last couple of years, in order to get things back on track." But in order to follow through on that vote, Soffran wants to hear a positive message and an agenda that inspires her—the kind Republicans failed to present in 2012.

As Steve Sareault surmises, New Hampshire independents have their own leanings, but they don't commit themselves quickly or easily. Republicans have a big opportunity after eight years of Obama to engage independents and press on their tendency to clean house and demand better. To take advantage of that opening, Republicans and conservatives will have to present themselves as a welcoming, and pragmatic, option to the status quo. That will take priority over specific issues and policy stances with independent voters in Hillsborough, New Hampshire.

GROUND GAME

In 2004, George Bush came within 10,000 votes[3] of winning New Hampshire, a narrow loss that reversed a 7,000-vote win in 2000.[4] Four years later, Republicans' fate in New Hampshire declined even more dramatically, with a loss by more than 68,000 for John McCain,[5] followed in 2012 by Mitt Romney's loss by almost 40,000 votes.[6]

Hillsborough, which holds almost a third of all New Hampshire voters, is the most competitive battleground in the Granite State. In all three cycles, the difference between

Republican and Democratic presidential contenders was less than 10,000 votes. However, the same issues that plagued McCain and Romney in Hillsborough played out in the rest of the state, with Hillsborough as the bellwether for strategic failure in New Hampshire.

What happened? Greg Moore, now a state director for Americans for Prosperity, said the Bush campaign had a muscular GOTV effort focused on Hillsborough and an economic message that worked in the county. "New Hampshire was doing pretty well in the middle part of the 2000s," Moore recalls. "At least this part of New Hampshire was." Four years later, the McCain campaign didn't have the resources to compete. "Mechanically, the McCain apparatus was nowhere near as strong as either the Obama campaign apparatus in 2008 or the Bush in 2004," Moore says. "That has to do with money and those resources, but that net [result] was McCain wasn't able to deliver the same type of turnout operation here in Manchester-Nashua and for that reason. . . . And it made a big difference," especially in the context of the 2008 financial-sector crisis and the early stages of the Great Recession.

In 2012, "Romney did a little bit better" but still couldn't compete with Obama on GOTV. Nor did that seem to be the focus, at least from Moore's position at the time as the chief of staff of the New Hampshire House. "The Romney operation was still more driven by message than actual boots on the ground, very different than Bush," Moore says. "Even though he got a higher set of numbers than McCain, the actual on-the-ground fieldwork was remarkably disparate."

In order to win in 2016, the GOP needs to reverse that

trend, getting on the ground to identify voters, their issues, and their prospective direction in the next election. This can't wait until the general election, either. "If you show up and just say I'm going to do GOTV, it's not going to get you very far," Moore advises. "If you knew nothing else and you landed from Mars, it would be a good strategy. But if you're actually trying to look at growing the pie the way the Obama operation has, that's the way you do it."

When asked in the summer of 2015 whether those efforts had begun, Moore replies, "I haven't seen it yet—let's put it that way." But he hasn't seen Democrats on the ground doing it either. "In 2004, Bush earned it. In 2008 and 2012, Obama earned it. The question for 2016 is who wants to earn it."

THE HISTORY CHANNEL

Eight years ago, the opportunity to make history by electing the first African American president resonated powerfully across America, creating a strong emotional connection between voters and the Democratic candidate. Obama combined that emotional connection with a superior ground game and a general sense of fatigue with the old order of politics to become a once-in-a-generation politician—an unbeatable force in 2008. Even in 2012, by which time he looked beatable, Obama called on that emotional connection, keeping enough voters engaged to win a close reelection battle.

"In Obama's first election," Dave Scanlan recalls, "people were tired of what was going on in Iraq especially and Afghanistan. Obama was very articulate and charismatic, and people bought his ideology of change. They were looking for a different future." In 2012, Scanlan thinks the difference was the meat-grinder Republican primary, in which Mitt Romney emerged with significant damage.

The opportunity to make history doesn't explain the whole of Obama's success, but it clearly represented part of his emotional appeal. It did for Mike Conley, who cast his first presidential vote in the 2008 election as a college student. "At that time I was behind the idea of a little bit different president," he says now. "He was a black president, and I thought that was a good idea. Different point of view. What could that do for us?" Four years later, Conley was somewhat disappointed in Obama's performance, but the young man stuck with Obama, in part because of that "residual" emotional connection to the hope he felt during the 2008 campaign.

Cheryl, a young Manchester voter who prefers to use her first name only, saw the same dynamic with her friends, who wanted to give Obama more time despite being disappointed in his first-term performance. "They said, 'Well, he's only had four years and he needs four more to make what he said was going to happen, happen,'" she recalls. Even one friend who she thought had been convinced to vote for Romney changed his mind at the last minute, to Cheryl's chagrin. "I had him, just in conversations at work, I probably had him 60 percent convinced that he should vote for Romney instead," she says. But he changed his mind at the polling station. When Cheryl asked why, "It was the exact same answer. 'He needs more time.'"

In 2016, some Republicans worry that they may have to

run against history a second time, in the form of Hillary Clinton, who is vying again to become the first female president. Having watched the nation embrace a young and charismatic Obama as a symbol of social progress, the GOP can be forgiven for getting nervous over the prospect of doing it all over again. However, voters in Hillsborough clearly don't see the choice in those same terms.

Jeanine Soffran doesn't, regardless of her independent status. When asked about foreign policy, the topic of Hillary Clinton comes up, and Soffran shrugs off Clinton's experience as secretary of state. "I don't really have an opinion of it [Clinton's track record] one way or another," she tells me. Her response about the historical appeal of Clinton's candidacy is more direct. "Nope. Not at all. Zero." In her circle of female friends, Soffran says, Clinton's gender "doesn't matter. . . . Any woman would be thrilled to have the *right* woman president," Soffran says. "She is *not*."

Kevin Healey, a firefighter and a lifelong Democrat with teenagers at home, relates a recent experience he had at a hair salon. "I was sitting and getting my hair cut and there were six or seven women, aging from age thirty-five to about sixty," Healey says. "They were talking about politics. And I said, oh here we go. First thing out of their mouth was Hillary Clinton. I expected them to say, well we like Hillary Clinton because of X, Y, and Z."

Healey, however, was in for a surprise. "There wasn't a woman, not one, in that whole room that was going to vote for Hillary Clinton. I didn't ask why. I didn't say anything. I just let them talk. And they said, 'We don't want to be the only woman that votes for Hillary Clinton because she's a woman. If we don't believe in what she's saying, then we're not going to vote for her.' "

So who did they prefer at this point, several months before the primaries? "I let the conversation go, and they said, one of them, well who are you voting for? They said, 'I really like . . . *Donald Trump.*' "

This underscores the real opportunity Republicans have to push for independents in 2016. In this cycle, the Democratic opponent matters less than the GOP's own candidate— matters less than his or her ability to connect with these voters. This will require a campaign that understands that demographics are not necessarily destiny, one that fights for votes rather than assuming that the current of history may have locked a set of voters away from them.

YOUTH MOVEMENTS—UP AND OUT?

Young voters made up a major part of the Obama coalition in 2008 and in 2012. According to the exit polls for New Hampshire in 2008,[7] Obama won the state's eighteen- to twenty-nine-year-old demographic by a 61/37 margin—although he actually won *all* age demographics here on his way to a 54/45 win over John McCain. Still, young voters accounted for 18% of the vote and provided the widest margin by far of all the demos.

Four years later, Obama's overall margin of victory narrowed to 52/46 in New Hampshire, but he actually gained a percentage point among younger voters, 62/34.[8] College-age voters turned out to be among the most resilient slice of

Obama's coalition in New Hampshire, breaking even stronger in 2012 than in 2008.*

To win New Hampshire in 2016, Republicans need to compete better among younger voters. Winning this demographic matters less in terms of overall victory than it does in helping to keep the gap narrow. Democrats, on the other hand, are tasked with both keeping younger voters from leaving the coalition and ensuring that they turn out like they did in the last two elections for Obama.

How, then, can Republicans compete for those votes? In large part, they need to show up and engage with students and graduates who are in the early stages of their professional lives. Mike Conley, whose only presidential votes have gone to Obama, attended a Scott Walker campaign event and came away impressed with the Wisconsin governor. Conley, whose six-foot-five height can cause some to feel intimidated in his presence, was impressed with Walker's poise.

"Being cognizant of being taller than everybody else, I try to be as calm and collected as possible," Conley says about his approach to these events. "I went up to Scott, and I said, 'Sir, I'm Mike Conley. I just wanted to wish you the best of luck. And it was a pleasure to hear you speak today.' Most people will just shake my hand and be like, oh yeah, thank

---

* College-age students, a subset of this demographic (eighteen to twenty-four years of age), voted for Obama by roughly the same margin as the eighteen to twenty-nine demo, 62/37, and accounted for 10% of the overall New Hampshire vote. Four years later, the same demographic (but likely not the same voters, given the narrow age parameters) voted slightly stronger for Obama, 67/30, with that narrower age demo accounting for 12% of the vote.

you very much and walk away." But Walker treated Conley differently—he took a moment to connect. "He pulled me closer and looked me in the eye. I was thrown back somewhat. Here's a guy who is able to look up to me and not look uncomfortable. He stood there and shook my hand firmly, and said a few nice words, and then went on his way."

What did that tell Conley about Walker? "I feel like a person that could do what Scott Walker did could handle things different, as far as foreign policy." Walker also impressed Conley with his ability to articulate positions and wants to see that in a presidential candidate. "That's a person to me that shows they've done the research. They know what they're talking about."

Most of all, Conley looks for a candidate who is oriented to the future rather than the past. Unlike some conservatives, he wants to see government invest in innovation, especially when it comes to eliminating environmental problems. At the same time, he wants a president who will focus on lowering the national debt. Conley remembers hearing the president talk about dealing with the national debt, but Obama argued that "in order to get out of debt, we had to spend more. And the debt doubled," Conley recalls. "That scared me. It needs to be fixed."

The future is a big concern for Cheryl, too, especially in terms of economic policies. Like Conley, Cheryl worries about the national debt, but that worry is directed more specifically at the burden it places on future economic growth. She says this concern springs from the fact that she has started her career and is beginning to see marriage and family as more solid, near-term goals.

"I'm not right out of high school, and I'm not right out of college," Cheryl says. "Now it's playing a bigger factor, because I'm getting older, and I want to make sure that what we're doing now is going to benefit the next generation. So when I have kids, it's not some chaos that I'm going to leave them with."

The quality of the candidate matters more to Cheryl than having the perfect policy agenda, at least in terms of inspiration and motivation to evangelize for a candidate. A big key to this is a sense that the candidate understands who the voters are and identifies with their struggle. This means sharing a concern for the future with Cheryl and others in her generation who have begun to invest in it.

Millennials aren't the only ones worrying about future generations. The slowing rate of population growth in Hillsborough reflects the end of an influx, and perhaps an outflow of Hillsborough's younger generation. This outflow is directly related to a quality-of-life issue that hits home in a very personal—and very literal—way.

Hillsborough residents tend to be better educated than the national average, with a higher percentage of high school graduates (90.8% compared with 86% nationally) and college graduates (35% to 28.8%).[9] While the unemployment rate in the county remains low at 3.8%, job growth has plateaued.[10]

When the sons and daughters of Hillsborough County parents graduate—either from college or high school—the opportunities to make a life at home seem fewer and less attainable. "Everybody's kids are moving out," Patrick Hynes says. "Everybody. They graduate from college, and they move somewhere else to find a job." As a result, parents face a future of having their children move far away, and this feeds into their wider frustration with economic stagnation.

If presidential candidates want to connect to voters in a visceral, personal way, Hynes advises them to pay attention to this anxiety. "It's depressing in a you-love-your-home-state thing," Hynes says, "but it's also depressing because parents want to be close to their kids and then eventually their grandkids, and there's a sense of 'We're missing out.'" This is where the pragmatic, independent quality of New Hampshire voters will express itself rather than get tangled up in national messaging. "[Candidates] who will talk in specifics about economic growth are going to [find] a ready ear," Hynes says, "as opposed to ideological appeals."

Kevin Healey expresses similar fears for the future of his four children, two of whom are in college and one of whom will go in the next couple of years. "Being an Irish-born family, my parents always said to me, pay your bills, work hard, and save your money, and things are going to work for you. Well, that's not really the case anymore," he says. "I saved my money and I worked very hard and I paid my bills, and at the end of the day, I still struggle like anyone else because I get 2 percent on my money at the bank, but I pay 8 percent to Sallie Mae for my kids' student loans. So I turn around and I say, wow, how can this possibly be? Why is it I'm only getting 2 percent but the government is charging me 8? Why can't they make it more financially feasible for these kids and for us as parents?"

Neil Levesque, executive director of the New Hampshire Institute of Politics at Saint Anselm College, says this was an issue that Republicans largely ignored in the 2014 midterms, too, to the benefit of Democrats. "We had large groups of college students here who were interested in the student loan issue. And when they identified a candidate who they thought was going to help them on that," Levesque recalls, "they were going out and working in their office or in the streets."

Healey is working with his children to pay off their student loans, but he knows that many young people will have to shoulder that burden themselves. "So you have these kids who work hard, go to school, get into college, get a degree, come out with $100,000 in debt, can't find a job, only to be hit with 8 percent interest and then go into this vicious cycle." For the upcoming election, Healy is looking at both parties for a solution. "I don't care if you're Republican, Democrat, or independent," he says. "If you start singing my song, I'm going to listen."

Healey won't be alone. If Republicans want to make inroads with younger voters, they will need to address the economic issues that hit home with them: stagnant growth, staggering debt on both the personal and national level, and the structural issues that very well could cause them to enjoy a lower economic standard of living than that of their parents. And their parents will also be watching closely.

GOING RED IN THE GRANITE STATE

Hillsborough is the key to winning New Hampshire, and personal contact and shoe leather are the keys to winning Hillsborough. "We're used to getting down and meeting the candidates," Jayne Millerick says, and New Hampshire voters don't take campaigns seriously until they do. When they do meet the candidates, Millerick says, they want to see a positive, optimistic message and a sense of competence from the candidates. "The days where we can grouse in a room and talk to each other about all the bad things that are going on in this country and hope to get voters—that's not going to happen," Millerick emphasizes. "We've proven time and time again that is a plan that is destined for failure."

Why focus on New Hampshire at all? With only four Electoral College votes, its mathematical impact on the presidential contest is limited, at best. It has a more direct impact on the primaries. However, its diversity and accessibility make it a good laboratory for campaigns and candidates. The person who wins New Hampshire will likely have created a superior organization and learned how to effectively reach sophisticated and somewhat skeptical voters—especially independents. This quality matters not just in New Hampshire, but in every other swing county and swing state as well.

In order to turn New Hampshire red, the Republican candidate needs to put significant time into identifying voters like Kevin Healey and Mike Conley, who have never voted Republican but are now looking for a change of direction. They need to at least make the Sturms and Pete Basiliere feel comfortable with a potential choice of the GOP with a positive message and tone. They have an opportunity to reach younger voters like Conley and Cheryl, and parents like Healey, by understanding their concerns on the economy and explaining their agenda in the context of their lives, and not just relying on ideological or philosophical arguments about free markets. Most of all, the winning candidate will need to show voters like Jeanine Soffran that they want to make government work rather than use it to fight a series of ideological battles.

If the Republican candidate can do that in New Hampshire while staying faithful to their own ideals, Hillsborough and the state will be within their reach. The question for 2016, as Greg Moore says, is who wants to *earn* Hillsborough, the state, and the presidency.

CONCLUSION
LEARNING THE LESSON

S o, have Republicans learned the right lessons from 2012? And, more important, do they have a shot at winning in 2016? The feedback from the field is mixed.

Jorge Bonilla, who ran for Congress in Florida's critical I-4 Corridor, sees big improvements there from the RNC, and in Ohio, the difference has been "night and day," according to Hamilton County commissioner Greg Hartmann. "[RNC chairman Reince] Priebus has done a great job. He inherited a huge debt and shaky leadership," Hartmann notes. Priebus convinced the RNC's donors to invest in a candidate-independent presidential turnout machine, and the results can already be seen. "You've got to have the building blocks in place, and then you have to have a strong candidate that can run on those tracks. So we're in much better shape than we were in the past."

Priebus himself is confident in the RNC's preparations for the next cycle, saying that the findings from the 2012 "autopsy" will transform the way future campaigns are run.

"The way national parties have worked over the years is that we accumulate cash, we wait for a nominee, and then we spend that money," Priebus says. "But I can't show up in

Cleveland and Cincinnati for the first time in four years in September of 2016 and expect to have an impact on the community. So the basic premise of this is that if you are going to compete in Hispanic, black, or Asian communities, and compete better with veterans and people of faith, you have to work on it on a year-round basis."

If Republicans can do this, the GOP can stop strategizing for smaller turnouts and start driving the larger turnouts in the same way that the Barack Obama campaign did in 2008 and 2012. The Republican Leadership Initiative (RLI), an outgrowth of the Growth and Opportunity Project, shifts the organizational effort from the candidate to the party—and shifts the party effort from national to granular. This goes beyond demographics, Priebus argues, and all the way down to peer-to-peer politics.

"At the end of 2014, I think we had over 4,200 paid employees. When I walked in the door here, we had less than 80," Priebus says. The RLI "hire[s] people from the communities that we want to influence, from the community to stay in the community, to then meet metrics that we set," he explains. "That means one-on-one meetings for that community, and that means not just necessarily sitting around talking about fracking and clean coal; it means having a pizza party, bringing a band in, once in a while giving hot dogs out and talking to people, and then going to community events."

The RLI's efforts have focused on key counties, Priebus says, but they go even more granular than that—and into territory where Republicans have traditionally resisted investing. "If you're not in black and Hispanic communities hardly at all for four straight years, and then you go in and try to saturate those communities, certainly you're going to do better than you did before."

Getting people involved from these communities helps, Priebus says, because it establishes "a level of trust that is built over time in order for things to change for your future election results to the positive." A secondary benefit is that it helps to defend against dishonest attacks and media-driven outrage over fringe statements. "If you don't represent the community otherwise, you have no one that is there at the church festival on Sunday or the community event to say, *hey wait a second, hang on—this is what Republicans believe.*"

The RNC isn't aiming for immediate victories in these previously unengaged communities as much as they are to gain ground. "I don't know what the numbers are off the top of my head," Priebus says, "but I'm sure they're anywhere from 2 to 5 percent in the black community of Milwaukee, which is terrible." But if Republicans can go from 5% to 10% to 12%, "that's when you make a huge difference" in election outcomes.

In hotly contested places like Prince William, such an increase could put Republicans in position to win the county and the state. In his reelection bid in Ohio, John Kasich got an extraordinary 26% of African American votes; in 2016, even half of that performance would win the state for the Republican nominee.

While much of this sounds as though it follows the lessons from Barack Obama's two massively successful organizing efforts—and in large part it does—there is one key difference. Until now, both parties largely left this kind of structural organization to the candidates. The Democratic

National Committee did not run the organizing efforts in 2008 or 2012, and one key question heading into 2016 is whether the next Democratic nominee can commit both the resources and the inspiration to duplicate it.

Priebus wants to lift that burden from the candidate by building a turnkey operation that can coordinate with the eventual nominee, no matter who he or she is. "The fact is," Priebus says, "when you've got sixteen candidates, they're raising money to win a nomination fight in Iowa, New Hampshire, and South Carolina. They are not necessarily worried about how many voter registrations we're picking up in Florida, Ohio, or Nevada. That's our problem."

Of course, the candidate would have to decide whether to use this RNC turnkey organization, but as Priebus says, they would have to be crazy to pass it up. "We sit down with the nominee and say, *here you go*. We've not only got our finances straight, we've got the $26 million waiting in the presidential trust for you," Priebus says. "We've got this field operation with this many thousands or however many the amount of people. We got a data operation that is something that we can be proud of. We've got our act together when it comes to our digital operation as well. That's what a competent national party needs to be able to do."

This may be the Democrats' Achilles' heel in 2016. While cautioning that he has no special insight into DNC operations, Priebus believes that they remain candidate-driven in organization. "The [Republican] candidates running for president look to the RNC as being the place that has to build these things, because no one else is in the hard-money world that we're in," Priebus says. "The DNC is built around a candidate. So the DNC is not necessarily the place that is going to build the best data file, and they are not the place that is going to build the ground game."

That may not matter for Hillary Clinton, who raised a large amount of money for organizing purposes well ahead of the primary process. If Democrats nominate someone else, it will become a real problem. "One of the challenges a guy like Joe Biden [would have had]," Priebus says, "is that if he can't build it, he has to rely on a hard-money committee to do it for him. He doesn't have it."

Echoing Priebus, *Pittsburgh Tribune-Review* reporter Salena Zito notes that the RNC has indeed begun gaining traction in key communities early enough to make a difference in 2016. "I've seen the RNC do it in Ohio, West Virginia, and Pennsylvania, and Colorado. They've done a really good job. If you look in Pennsylvania or Ohio, they already have hundreds of people deployed on the ground, doing this kind of stuff in anticipation of 2016. That's really important."

They have begun in Prince William County, too, Zito says. "I'm pretty sure they have one of those block programs, several block programs, right in Prince William County. Part of the problem is people watch too much national news," Zito says about the lack of attention to this infrastructure building by the RNC, "but if you pay attention to the local news, that's where you see them doing this."

Sara Remini, a Young Republican in North Carolina's Wake County who called the GOP's ground game in 2012 "an utter failure," sees reason for hope in 2016. "The RNC is starting to develop a better technology," Remini says, "probably with the 2012 election and a lot since then, where we've got better software and better capability of door knocking and everything. This is still relatively new for the Republican Party, so actually getting people to use this and transcend this new way of doing things, it's going to go through some growing pains. I think we're still in that growing pains stage. We need to amp up for 2016, which is right around the corner."

Remini's right: 2016 is "right around the corner," and it may be the last chance for conservatives to correct the course of the nation before the Obama-progressive track becomes a permanent baseline. But in this election, there's reason to believe that the GOP won't be fighting empty-handed.

AN INFLECTION ELECTORATE FOR AN INFLECTION-POINT ELECTION

My travels through these seven battleground counties revealed a good news/bad news situation for Republicans as they approach November 2016. The bad news is that the old days of GOP dominance in these swing counties and states on the strength of culture and history alone are over. Not only have times changed, but so have the voters in these counties, with migration patterns and economic shifts making it more difficult to earn their trust. The Republican Party must adapt to those changes or become irrelevant, and 2012 showed us that if the GOP wants to avoid that fate, it has a lot of work to do.

The good news is a little more complex. The 2012 election in these former Republican strongholds demonstrates that the United States may not be a conservative or even center-right nation all on its own. However, the conservative/ Republican message still can compete for votes—as long as Republicans actually show up to *compete* for them.

Perhaps the voters in these battlegrounds can best be described as the inflection electorate in an inflection-point election. After eight years of increasingly sharp progressive shifts in governance, voters are looking for a change of direction. Obama's retirement from politics removes both his organizational and inspirational impact on voters, allowing for a fresh start and a requirement for both parties to orient themselves toward the future. The victory will go to the party and candidate adapting most quickly and effectively to the electorate as it is, not as they wish it to be.

The best news for Republicans and conservatives is that the RNC has decided, as Priebus says above, to give the nominee a head start. If Priebus succeeds, then the turnkey operation only needs the right kind of campaign and candidate to engage voters and expand the reach of conservative and Republican policies. The primary offered a multitude of choices to Republican voters, but the eventual nominee must understand what it will take to win these battlegrounds, no matter who he or she may be.

What *will* it take to win? Three qualities came across most clearly in all seven battleground counties. First, voters want a principled but pragmatic approach to governance. As Lou Terhar, the state representative from Hamilton County, Ohio, says, "Politics to me is not nearly as smoke and mirror-y as people like to make it out. . . . What's going to work? How do you attack the problem? Give me something I understand."

Carolina Journal's John Hood emphasizes that pragmatism is not a call for moderation, but a "way to attract people . . . because they feel like somebody's solving their problems."

Next, optimism wins out for voters in these battlegrounds. "The days where we can grouse in a room and talk to each other about all the bad things that are going on in this country and hope to get voters" are over, former New Hampshire Republican State Committee chair Jayne Millerick insists. "We need a candidate who not only has a positive message but can talk to people in a tone that they know first of all they've got their best interests at heart, even if they don't agree with them on every issue."

Finally, voters want to know that the candidate understands them and has empathy for their concerns. Tone plays a key part in this as well, not just to certain demographics but applied consistently. "Genuineness and humility matter," advises Wisconsin congressman Reid Ribble about Brown County voters. "You've got to be able to bring people together, rather than pushing them apart. If your entire campaign is built on separation rather than uniting, you're going to be in trouble in Brown County."

The direct method of expressing that empathy is engagement. The RNC is setting up the mechanism for the eventual nominee, but that candidate needs to be willing to use it, and to listen to those who know the voters. "If the national [candidate] would listen to people who do already know the communities, you could bypass the need to learn about [them]," says former Virginia attorney general Ken Cuccinelli. "You got to bring it down to people's kitchen table. They've got to understand how it matters in their life."

In the end, politics is simply the mechanism by which human beings navigate the issues within communities. We get cynical about politics because of how practitioners conduct it, but politics in its essential form is the art of public relationships. Data inform it, communications media can help make connections to extend it, and segmentation can assist in shepherding resources for it—but none of these is a replacement for person-to-person contact. Too often, and certainly in the last two Republican presidential campaigns, public relations have replaced public relationships. Too often, the exchange of ideas has became a one-way, top-down lecture rather than a conversation between peers. In order to succeed in politics within any kind of community—a nonprofit, a corporation, a club, or a nation—one must build public relationships by recognizing the need for both sides to know each other.

The real opportunities for conservatives and Republicans shown in *Going Red* have implications far beyond 2016. Getting this right will put the GOP on the path to victory in November, but its effects will ripple much further into the future. Building relationships with voters, especially in communities where Republicans have a history of neglect or abandonment, will strengthen their ability to evangelize for conservative principles and to defend themselves. But it also has the ability to heal and lift up American politics to a more humane and substantive level—which is why the GOP must follow through on these efforts past 2016, even if the immediate results seem marginal.

Perhaps the greatest irony in this potential is that the GOP will have that opportunity because they got clobbered by Hope and Change in 2008 and 2012. Republicans have the ability to facilitate exactly that outcome, not by creating a national cult of personality surrounding one political figure, but by making the Republican and conservative agenda relevant to each of these communities, and therefore making the American people the true focus of the campaign—in practice and not just in rhetoric. That would not be just a Republican victory, but a win for everyone, and worthy of the promise of a democratic republic.

ACKNOWLEDGMENTS

Every book tells a story, and every book has its own story. This book's story began at the Conservative Political Action Conference in March 2015, when I offered to fill in for my friend and colleague Katie Pavlich on the last panel discussion at the annual conservative event in DC. The topic was the 2016 election and what Republicans and conservatives needed to do to win it. Thanks to a need to fill time while the CPAC staff calculated the results of the straw poll, we got to talk a lot longer than planned. Colleagues of Crown Forum happened to be in the audience, and editor Derek Reed contacted me shortly afterward to ask whether I might be interested in taking a concept he had for a book and making it a reality.

Every book has an author, but every book has a long list of people who make it possible. Within weeks, Derek and his team worked with me to develop a workable book proposal that had everyone excited, including Penguin Random House senior vice president and publisher Tina Constable. Throughout the process of writing *Going Red,* the entire Crown team provided solid support, but Derek has been a great coach, cheerleader, and, of course, editor.

Most first-time authors know next to nothing about book publishing, and this author was no exception. When it came time to make the deal, I had Mel Berger at William Morris Entertainment to represent me, and I'm glad I did. My friend Jim Geraghty introduced us, and Bernard Goldberg kindly took time in between flights to urge me to go with his long-time agent. Kathleen Breaux and David Hinds in Mel's office have been kind and helpful along the way.

The key to this book rested on identifying the counties to profile for the 2016 election. Karl Rove and his team supplied me with their extensive data based on the profile I wanted—swing-state counties that Republicans won in 2004 but lost in 2008 and 2012. Duane Patterson, my good friend and pro-ducer extraordinaire of *The Hugh Hewitt Show* on the Salem Radio Network, introduced me to Karl's chief of staff Kristin Davison at Karl Rove & Company in Washington, DC. She became my data guru, giving me a list of nearly three dozen counties to research. And when it came time to apply that re-search, Paul Westcott and the team at L2 VoterMapping gave me access to their granular data and the precinct maps that allowed me to accurately identify specific neighborhoods. Their assistance made my work much easier, and made it pos-sible to work on the tight deadlines this project required.

A number of people deserve recognition for the critical roles they played in making contact with people in these counties. James Hewitt and Raffi Williams at the RNC found local party officials and officeholders. Katy Abrams at Ameri-cans for Prosperity and Brian Faughnan at the LIBRE Ini-tiative put me in contact with local activists. Conservative radio hosts such as Jerry Bader in Green Bay, Wisconsin, and

Pudgy Miller in Raleigh, North Carolina, made key introductions to grassroots activists and voters; Pudgy even pulled together a great luncheon conference where a few of us hashed out the challenges of the world and still had time for the meal. Chuck McGee of Spectrum Marketing offered me office space in Manchester and arranged several meetings with voters in the area. Markeece Young invited me to a Young Republicans meet-and-greet in Raleigh that turned out to be particularly important for my work in that community.

Getting around in unfamiliar territory can be challenging, even in an era of GPS-equipped rental cars. Maggi Cook in Ohio and Mitch Kokai in North Carolina gave me extensive tours of their counties that helped me understand the local geography and cultural delineations.

A few old friends came through for me, too. Patrick Hynes of Hynes Communications and I go way back in the blogging world, and he helped give me the lay of the land. Kelly Maher of Compass Colorado not only made introductions but also gave me work and meeting space, plus offered constant encouragement. Jon Ham, the father of my friend and colleague Mary Katharine Ham, made introductions for me in Wake County. Kevin Binversie helped make more contacts in Wisconsin from his perch at LakeshoreLaments.com; Nick Mascari did the same in Ohio, and Mickey White in Virginia. Tom and Sally Schmidt housed us at Sabamba, their B&B and alpaca farm in De Pere, Wisconsin, a wonderful place to relax for a few days or to use as a base of operations. My good friend Jolinda Conzemius provided the portrait photograph for this book.

Most of the people who made those arrangements also

had their voices included in *Going Red*. Not so Susan Abel, who found at least half of the contacts I had in Prince William County, Virginia. Susan kindly called on a number of people she knew, despite only knowing me through my work at HotAir.com, and helped me connect with numerous people on the local scene. Susan does not live or work in Prince William County, but her insight was invaluable, and her efforts made this a better book. Similarly, my good friend Lorie Byrd helped me understand Wake County and its politics, as well as its barbecue.

When it came time to work with the interviews, my colleague and good friend Jazz Shaw and his wife, Georg-Karen Hawks, played a critical role in making them usable on a short schedule. The two of them did a great job transcribing the interviews from my recordings, shaving untold weeks off the necessary time to write the book. Many of these conversations took place in loud environments, but only occasionally would I see comments inserted into the transcript such as this: SMALL CHILD YELLS "YEAH!" IN THE BACKGROUND REPEATEDLY AND MAKES ME WANT TO HUNT HIM OR ED WITH A SPORK. The spork hunt would have been justified, I assure you, and I would have gladly traded it for the fine work Jazz and Georg-Karen did.

Speaking of my colleagues and friends, I am extremely grateful for Jazz and Allahpundit, my fellow editors at HotAir.com. They helped cover for me while I traveled, trying to juggle my normal workload and the book at the same time, and made it possible for me to essentially work two full-time jobs. This book could not have been written without their assistance. I'd also like to offer a special thanks to Mary

Katharine Ham, our editor at large and Fox News contributor, who was prepared to revamp her schedule to cover for my complete absence when it came time to do the heavy lifting for the final drafting of the book. Her beloved husband, Jake Brewer, died suddenly as the result of an accident during a bike rally to raise money for cancer research. Our hearts are still broken for MK and her two children.

On our Townhall.com side, my boss Jonathan Garthwaite cheered and supported me in this endeavor from the very beginning. I got great advice and encouragement from my friends Guy Benson and Katie Pavlich, both also bestselling authors and Fox News contributors who pointed out a couple of potential pitfalls early on. Amanda Muñoz, Matt Vespa, Christine Rousselle, Cortney O'Brien, Storm Paglia, and others provided support for me as well. Hugh Hewitt and Duane Patterson from Salem Radio Network have long been good friends and mentors, as has my good friend, blogger, and author Andrew Malcolm.

While I traveled and wrote, we had a number of guest bloggers fill in for us, making it possible for me to have the maximum amount of flexibility. Bruce McQuain, Matt Vespa, Gabriel Malor, Taylor Millard, Kristina Ribali, Allan Bourdius, C. T. Rex, and Amanda Muñoz have all graciously given their time and effort to help out and contribute to HotAir .com.

Writing this book took me on the road for months, for which I needed the support of my family most of all. My son, David, daughter-in-law, Melissa, and granddaughters, Kayla and Elizabeth, put up with me missing family events with patience and understanding. My mother, Barbara, my father,

Ed Sr., and his wife, Doris, and my sister, Cindie, all cheered me on to success. Most of all, my wife, Marcia, has been my rock, my sounding board, and my inspiration. Every word I write, here and on HotAir.com and other outlets, is possible only with the partnership she has provided me ever since I launched my writing career more than twelve years ago.

Finally, my greatest gratitude goes to the people who generously gave of their time and experience to inform me about their lives, their concerns, and their communities. Most of them show up in the book; a few do not, in order to keep the pacing in the discussion. In most cases, they gave me not just their attention but their friendship. Over the last five months, I feel as though I made more friends than at any other similar time frame in my life.

As I have written this book, I have felt the heavy responsibility for telling their stories properly, presenting their communities accurately, and allowing them to provide readers with the insight to understand their unique identities within the electorate. These are their stories, not mine. Thank you all for your trust, your kindness, your hospitality, and your friendship.

NOTES

INTRODUCTION

1. CBS News Twitter feed, "Barack Obama Re-elected as President of the United States," https://twitter.com/CBSNews/status/266031103763161089.
2. Noah Rothman, "Obama Reveals to *Entertainment Tonight* Details of His Relationship with George Clooney," *Mediaite,* http://www.mediaite.com/tv/obama-reveals-to-entertainment-tonight-details-of-his-relationship-with-george-clooney/.
3. *Washington Post Election Day Live Blog* (link dead), via HotAir.com, http://hotair.com/archives/2012/11/06/7-p-m-ohio-virginia-north-carolina/.
4. Sam Stein on Twitter, https://twitter.com/samsteinhp/statuses/265974859530633216.
5. GOP.com, "Growth & Opportunity Project," http://goproject.gop.com/.
6. Ibid.
7. Ibid., "Messaging," p. 4.
8. Drew DeSilver, "Ahead of Redistricting, Democrats Seek to Reverse Statehouse Declines," Pew Research, http://www.pewresearch.org/fact-tank/2015/03/02/ahead-of-redistricting-democrats-seek-to-reverse-statehouse-declines/.
9. MultiState Associates Incorporated, "2015 Governors and

Legislatures," https://www.multistate.com/state-resources /governors-legislatures.

10. CNN, 2004 Election Results, http://www.cnn.com/ELEC TION/2004/pages/results/president/.

11. CNN, 2012 Election Results Exit Polls, http://www.cnn.com /election/2012/results/race/president/.

12. Ibid.

13. Michael D. Shear, "Demographic Shift Brings New Worry for Republicans," *New York Times*, November 7, 2012, http:// www.nytimes.com/2012/11/08/us/politics/obamas-victory -presents-gop-with-demographic-test.html?_r=0.

14. Peter Wehner, "The GOP Is Killing Itself," *Commentary*, September 22, 2015, https://www.commentarymagazine.com /politics-ideas/campaigns-elections/gop-nativism-2016/.

15. John Ziegler, "Trump-Fueled Media Circus Causing an Epic Conservative Crackup," *Mediaite*, September 22, 2015, http://www.mediaite.com/online/trump-fueled-media -circus-causing-an-epic-conservative-crackup/.

FLORIDA

1. US Census Bureau, Estimate for Zip Code 33647 in 2000, http://factfinder.census.gov/faces/tableservices/jsf/pages /productview.xhtml?src=CF.

2. US Census Bureau, Estimate for Zip Code 33647 in 2010, http://factfinder.census.gov/faces/tableservices/jsf/pages /productview.xhtml?src=CF.

3. University of Michigan Population Studies Center, from US Census Bureau data, http://www.psc.isr.umich.edu/dis /census/Features/tract2zip/index.html.

4. US Census Bureau, Quick Facts, http://quickfacts.census .gov/qfd/states/12/12057.html.

5. "The Price for the Heights," *City Times*, June 11, 2004. http://

www.sptimes.com/2004/06/11/Citytimes/The_price_for
_the_Hei.shtml.

OHIO

1. "Ohio's History in Presidential Elections," OhioElection
Results.com, http://ohioelectionresults.com/documents/Pres
idential/Ohio%20Presidential%20Analysis.pdf.
2. Ohio Electoral College history, 270toWin.com. http://www
.270towin.com/states/Ohio.
3. Ibid.
4. CNN, "Democrats Challenge Ohio Electoral Votes," January 6, 2005, http://www.cnn.com/2005/ALLPOLITICS/01
/06/electoral.vote.1718/index.html.
5. US Election Atlas, http://uselectionatlas.org/RESULTS
/index.html.
6. Ibid.
7. "Cincinnatus," Mount Vernon Library, http://www.mount
vernon.org/research-collections/digital-encyclopedia
/article/cincinnatus/.
8. Tracy L. Kamerer and Scott W. Nolley, "Rediscovering an
American Icon," *Colonial Williamsburg Journal*, Autumn 2003,
http://www.history.org/foundation/journal/autumn03
/houdon.cfm.
9. Cincinnati Museum FAQ, http://library.cincymuseum.org
/cincifaq.htm.
10. US Census Bureau, Decennial Census Figures, http://www
.census.gov/en.html.
11. US Census Bureau, Quick Facts, http://www.census.gov
/quickfacts/table/INC110213/00,39,39061,3915000.
12. Dann Woellert, *The Authentic History of Cincinnati Chili*
(April 2013), pp. 9–10, https://books.google.com/books?id
=B6mh0iOdtWYC&pg=PA10&hl=en#v=onepage&q&f=false.

13. Randy A. Simes, "Gentrification Occurring in More Than Cincinnati's Center City Neighborhoods," *UrbanCincy*, December 23, 2013, http://www.urbancincy.com/2013/12/gentrification-occurring-in-more-cincinnati-neighborhoods-than-just-those-in-center-city/.

14. Maggie Haberman and Alexander Burns, *Politico*, "Romney's ORCA program sank," November 9, 2012, http://www.politico.com/story/2012/11/romneys-orca-program-sank-083653.

15. US Census Bureau, Quick Facts, April 2014 estimates (latest available at time of writing), http://www.census.gov/quickfacts/table/INC110213/00,39,39061,3915000.

16. Ibid; 2010 data used, as no later estimates were available.

17. "2014 Ohio Governor Election Results," *Politico*, http://www.politico.com/2014-election/results/map/governor/ohio/#.VfmdRZ1VhBc.

18. "Lighting a Revolution," Smithsonian Institute, http://americanhistory.si.edu/lighting/history/patents/mosbyl.htm.

NORTH CAROLINA

1. 966,889 Democratic to 973,206 Republican voters.

2. "Mad Money: TV Ads in the 2012 Presidential Campaign," *Washington Post*, undated, http://www.washingtonpost.com/wp-srv/special/politics/track-presidential-campaign-ads-2012/?tid=rr_mod.

3. US Census Bureau, Intercensal Estimates, April 2000–July 2010,http://www.census.gov/popest/data/intercensal/county/CO-EST00INT-01.html.

4. US Census Bureau, Cumulative Estimates of Resident Population Change and Rankings, April 2010–July 2014, http://factfinder.census.gov/faces/tableservices/jsf/pages/productview.xhtml?src=bkmk.

5. US Census Bureau, Quick Facts, Wake County, http://quick facts.census.gov/qfd/states/37/37183.html.

6. Reid Wilson, "27 Other Things the North Carolina Voting Law Changes," *Washington Post,* September 8, 2013, http://www .washingtonpost.com/blogs/govbeat/wp/2013/09/08/27 -other-things-the-north-carolina-voting-law-changes/.

7. Henry Gannett, *The Origin of Certain Place Names in the United States,* 2d ed. (Washington: Government Printing Office, 1905), p. 71; Town of Cary official website, http://www.town ofcary.org/newtocary/About_Cary/Looking_Back.htm.

8. US Census Bureau, Decennial Census Figures, http://www .census.gov/prod/www/abs/decennial/.

VIRGINIA

1. Virginia Electoral College history, 270toWin.com, http:// www.270towin.com/states/Virginia.

2. CNN, 2004 Election Results, http://www.cnn.com /ELECTION/2004/pages/results/states/VA/.

3. CNN, 2008 Election Results, http://edition.cnn.com /ELECTION/2008/results/state/#VA.

4. CNN, 2012 Election Results, http://www.cnn.com/election /2012/results/state/VA/president/.

5. Michael D. Shear, "Demographic Shift Brings New Worry for Republicans," *New York Times,* November 7, 2012, http:// www.nytimes.com/2012/11/08/us/politics/obamas-victory -presents-gop-with-demographic-test.html?_r=0.

6. "Virginia Gov: Cuccinelli vs. McAuliffe vs. Sarvis," Real-ClearPolitics, http://www.realclearpolitics.com/epolls/2013 /governor/va/virginia_governor_cuccinelli_vs_mcauliffe _vs_sarvis-4111.html#polls.

7. "Legislation Creating Prince William County, Virginia," Historic Prince William, http://www.historicprincewilliam.org /creation.html.

8. "Revolutionary War Campaign of 1781," Historical Marker Database, http://www.hmdb.org/marker.asp?marker=522.

9. US Census Bureau, Decennial Census Figures, http://www .census.gov/prod/www/decennial.html.

10. "Highest Income Counties in 2011," *Washington Post,* undated, http://www.washingtonpost.com/wp-srv/special/local /highest-income-counties/.

11. County of Prince William, Virginia, Comprehensive Annual Financial Report for the Fiscal Year Ended June 30, 2014, http:// www.pwcgov.org/government/dept/finance/Documents /FY%202014%20Comprehensive%20Annual%20Financial %20Report.pdf.

12. "Virginia Senate—Gillespie vs. Warner," RealClearPolitics, http://www.realclearpolitics.com/epolls/2014/senate/va /virginia_senate_gillespie_vs_warner-4255.html.

13. CNN, 2014 Virginia election results, http://www.cnn.com /election/2014/results/state/VA.

14. CNN, exit polls for Virginia from 2012, 2014.

15. Todos Supermarket website, http://www.todossupermarket .com/index.php?option=com_content&view=article&id=17 8&Itemid=467.

16. Amy Orndorff, "Residency Status Might Be Checked," *Washington Post,* June 28, 2007, http://www.washingtonpost.com /wp-dyn/content/article/2007/06/26/AR2007062602605 .html.

WISCONSIN

1. Dave Zirin, "Those Nonprofit Packers," *New Yorker,* January 25, 2011, http://www.newyorker.com/news/sporting-scene /those-non-profit-packers.

2. US Census Bureau, http://factfinder.census.gov/faces/nav /jsf/pages/community_facts.xhtml.

3. CNN, 2004 Election Results, http://www.cnn.com /ELECTION/2004/pages/results/states/WI/P/00/.
4. CNN, 2008 Election Results, http://edition.cnn.com /ELECTION/2008/results/individual/#mapPWI.
5. HuffPost Politics, Election Dashboard, http://elections .huffingtonpost.com/2012/wisconsin-recall-results.
6. CNN, 2012 Election Results, http://www.cnn.com/election /2012/results/state/WI/.

COLORADO

1. "The Blueprint," Rob Witwer and Adam Schrager, p. 6.
2. Ibid.
3. US Census Bureau, Quick Facts, from 2013 data, http://www.census.gov/quickfacts/table/INC110213 /00,08059,08,0803455.
4. Lynn Bartels, "Goodbye, Dear *Spot* Readers," *Denver Post*, July 25, 2015, http://blogs.denverpost.com/thespot /2015/07/25/goodbye-dear-spot-readers/122391/.
5. Luc Hatlestad, "Election Recap: Colorado Dems Feeling Mighty Blue," *5280*, November 5, 2014, http://www.5280.com /news/politics/digital/2014/11/election-recap-colorado -dems-feeling-mighty-blue.
6. Bruce Finley and Jesse Paul, "Animas River Spill: Hurdles Remain at Gold King," *Denver Post*, August 14, 2015, http:// www.denverpost.com/environment/ci_28638259/hurdles -remain-at-gold-king?source=hot-topic-bar.
7. "EPA: High Levels of Toxic Metal in Animas River Water after Mine Spill," CBS News, August 13, 2015, http://www.cbsnews .com/news/epa-high-toxic-metal-levels-in-animas-river-after -mine-spill/.
8. Ibid.
9. Noel Lyn Smith and Steve Garrison, "Top EPA Official

Observes Water Testing in Farmington," *Four Corners News,* August 13, 2015. http://www.daily-times.com/four_corners -news/ci_28625042/new-mexico-ag-meets-san-juan-county -leaders.

10. Jesse Paul, "Animas River Spill Makes Silverton Even Warier of EPA," *Denver Post,* August 15, 2015, http://www.denverpost .com/news/ci_28644587/spill-makes-silverton-even-warier -epa.

11. Ricardo Baca, "Colorado Pot Sales Spike in June, Top $50M for First Time," *Cannabist,* August 13, 2015, http://www .thecannabist.co/2015/08/13/colorado-marijuana-taxes -recreational-sales-june-2015-50-million/39384/?_ga=1.2321 29559.922741645.1438555125.

12. Katy Steinmetz, "These Five States Could Legalize Marijuana in 2016," *Time,* March 17, 2015, http://time.com/3748075 /marijuana-legalization-2016/.

13. Politico Election Central, "2014 Governor Election Results," http://www.politico.com/2014-election/results/map /governor/#.Vc_LWVNVhBc; "Jefferson County Election Results," *Denver Post,* http://data.denverpost.com/election /results/county/jefferson/2014/.

NEW HAMPSHIRE

1. "State Government Overview," *New Hampshire Almanac,* http://www.nh.gov/nhinfo/stgovt.html.

2. "Historical Census Browser," University of Virginia Library, http://mapserver.lib.virginia.edu/.

3. CNN, Elections Results in 2004, http://us.cnn.com /ELECTION/2004/pages/results/states/NH/P/00/.

4. US Election Atlas for the 2000 election, http://uselectionatlas .org/RESULTS/data.php?year=2000&datatype=national& def=1&f=0&off=0&elect=0.

5. CNN, Election Results for 2008, http://edition.cnn.com /ELECTION/2008/results/individual/#mapPNH.

6. CNN, Election Results for 2012, http://www.cnn.com /election/2012/results/state/NH/#president.

7. CNN, 2008 Exit Polls for New Hampshire, http://www.cnn .com/ELECTION/2008/results/polls/#NHP00p1.

8. CNN, 2012 Exit Polls for New Hampshire, http://www.cnn .com/election/2012/results/state/NH/#president.

9. US Census Bureau, Quick Facts, http://www.census.gov /quickfacts/table/INC110213/00,33,33011,3345140.

10. New Hampshire Employment Security, New Hampshire Local Area Unemployment Statistics, http://www.nhes.nh.gov/elmi /statistics/documents/nonseasonest.pdf.

INDEX